Kindergarten Standards

LEARNING BASIC VOCABULARY

Grade K

by
Marilee Woodfield

Published by Frank Schaffer Publications
an imprint of

McGraw Hill Children's Publishing

Author: Marilee Woodfield

 **Children's Publishing**

Published by Frank Schaffer Publications
An imprint of McGraw-Hill Children's Publishing
Copyright © 2004 McGraw-Hill Children's Publishing

Send all inquiries to:
McGraw-Hill Children's Publishing
3195 Wilson Drive NW
Grand Rapids, Michigan 49544

Kindergarten Standards for Learning Basic Vocabulary—grade K
ISBN: 0-7682-2810-7

1 2 3 4 5 6 7 8 9 PAT 09 08 07 06 05 04

The McGraw-Hill Companies

clock penny snowflake ✳ me 😊 apple 🍎

Table of Contents

triangle △   mother   eyes 👁 👁   planet 🪐   leaf 🍂

Introduction

In the 1840s, Friedrich Froebel's concerns for the education of young children was the genesis of modern-day kindergarten. *Kindergarten* literally means "a garden for children." He knew, as all kindergarten teachers know, that much like a garden, children need careful nurturing in order to grow and develop to their full potential. This requires a teacher dedicated to learning and an atmosphere that encourages individual growth on an appropriate level. The official position of ACEI concerning kindergarten states, "The Association for Childhood Education International recognizes the importance of kindergarten education and supports high-quality kindergarten programs that provide developmentally, culturally, and linguistically appropriate experiences for children." (Moyer, Egertson, and Isenberg, 1987) (http://www.acei.org)

Kindergarten Standards—Learning Basic Vocabulary provides themed activities and lessons centered around basic vocabulary words for kindergartners. Standards for the individual activities are taken from National Science Education standards, from NTCM principles and standards for school mathematics, and from recognized standards for language arts and social studies. The lessons and activities provide hands-on, classroom-tested activities. Whether it be reading stories about safety issues, experimenting with color words, or classifying animals, *Kindergarten Standards—Learning Basic Vocabulary* provides cross-curricular activities to promote understanding on many different levels.

Each themed lesson includes:

- **Words to Know**—The basic vocabulary words that are associated with that theme presented as age-appropriate learning experiences

- **Overview**—An at-a-glance look at the objectives of the lesson

- **Group Discussion**—Teaching and learning time for each theme and its associated vocabulary words

- **Independent Practice**—An opportunity for the children to try things on their own, dig a little deeper into the subject, and build on and reinforce the knowledge and skills they are mastering

- **Check for Understanding**—An opportunity to assess and evaluate the students' learning and comprehension of the subject matter

Additionally, at the back of this book, a set of flash cards are provided to help in labeling and word recognition with several of the vocabulary themes. In addition to the suggested uses in the lessons, you also may find additional ways to use them as teaching tools, such as lotto and matching games.

summer

flag

apple

me

snowflake

penny

clock

Standards Correlation Chart

Language Arts	Page #
Read a wide range of texts, literature and apply a variety of strategies to comprehend and interpret texts.	6, 21, 36, 39, 44, 63, 68, 73, 81, 90, 95, 105, 108, 111, 114, 117
Use spoken, written, and visual language to communicate effectively.	6, 7, 11, 29, 33, 36, 39, 42, 52, 63, 68, 81, 95, 108
Use spoken, written, and visual language to accomplish purposes.	29, 59

Social Studies	
Individual development and identity: explore factors that contribute to one's personal identity.	6, 11, 44, 61, 68
Express feelings related to different situations.	6, 29, 33, 68
Identify themselves as members of different groups and articulate similarities and differences between themselves and others.	6, 33, 44, 52, 59, 63, 68
Identify people at home or school with authority and what they do.	33, 36, 41, 44, 52, 63
Recognize surroundings, strangers, and areas of danger or risk.	36, 39, 41
Show caring and respect for others.	22, 52, 68, 83
Power, authority, and governance: Understand the purpose of government. Describe the rights and responsibilities of individuals and groups.	36, 44, 52, 59, 63

Math	
Demonstrate an understanding of the concept of time.	30, 90-92, 95-97, 100, 104
Use map and globe skills to determine the absolute location of places.	44, 63
Understand measurable attributes of objects and units of measurement.	55, 128
Recognize shapes in the environment and combine shapes to create two-dimensional objects.	81-83, 109
Understand concepts of ordinal numbers and their value.	6, 33, 40, 55, 87-88, 113
Understand various meanings and effects of addition and subtraction of whole numbers.	6, 55, 79, 105, 114
Understand patterns, relations, and functions through sorting, classifying, and ordering objects by size, number, and other properties.	11, 55, 73, 75, 81, 83, 105, 112, 135, 137
Select and use appropriate statistical methods to analyze data.	6, 75, 117

Science	
Observe common objects by using the five senses.	26, 73, 77, 81
Identify resources from Earth that are used in everyday life and understand that many resources can be conserved.	123-125
Materials can exist in different states.	28, 74, 115, 118, 123-124
Organisms have basic needs. Each plant or animal has different structures that serve different functions in growth, survival, and reproduction.	13, 19, 21, 44, 133-135, 136-138
Safety and security are basic needs of humans.	36, 39
Individuals have responsibility for their own health.	13, 19, 21
Weather changes from day to day and over the seasons.	100, 104, 105, 108, 111, 114, 117-119
Objects in the sky have patterns of movement.	117, 127
The sun provides the light and heat necessary to maintain the temperature of the earth.	111, 127, 133

triangle △   mother   eyes 👁👁   planet 🪐   leaf 🍂

 summer
 flag
 apple
 me
 snowflake
penny

All About Me

Words to know: me, unique, similar, different

Overview: All humans have similarities, but each one is a unique individual. Everyone has different interests and abilities.

100% YOU!

Materials: parent comment cards, tape recorder, large graph, marker

1. A few days before discussing this topic, send home a 3 x 5 card with a note requesting parents to write down three observations about their child. This could be things they like or dislike or a funny anecdote. Ask them to include their child's name on the card.

2. Read *I Like Me!,* by Nancy Carlson (Viking Press, 1988). Talk about how the pig is happy with herself just the way she is. Explain that we all have characteristics that are similar, but we are also unique, or different from, everyone else. Even identical twins, who often look exactly alike, have different interests, thoughts, and abilities. These differences are what make us unique and special. That is something to be proud of!

3. Gather the parent comment cards and pull one card from the stack. Explain to the children that you will be reading things that their parents have written about them. The children are to try to guess whom the comments are written about. After the comments have been read, guesses have been offered, and the child has been identified, have the entire class give that child a standing ovation and congratulate him or her on being "100% You!"

Extension: Have each child bring one special item from home to share with the class. This could be a favorite toy, a picture of a special occasion, a memento from a special event, etc. Line up all of the items along the front of the classroom and have each child write his or her name on a strip of paper to identify ownership of the items to create a "Me Museum."

 clock

0-7682-2810-7 *Learning Basic Vocabulary*

 clock penny snowflake me apple

Me Graphing

Materials: large graph sheet, markers, paper

The purpose of this activity is for the children to see how much they are like other children based on their likes and physical characteristics and how unique they are because of their own individual likes and differences.

1. Copy the list below—each concept on a separate 3 x 5 card. (You also may want to add or create your own.) With the children, talk about what *similar* and *different* mean. Talk about some of the obvious and not so obvious similarities/differences.

Similarities/Differences:

I like winter.	I like to sing.
I like summer.	I like to paint.
I like to eat pizza.	I like to play ball.
I like apples.	I like to read.
I like broccoli.	I can tie my shoe.

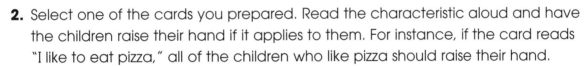

2. Select one of the cards you prepared. Read the characteristic aloud and have the children raise their hand if it applies to them. For instance, if the card reads "I like to eat pizza," all of the children who like pizza should raise their hand.

3. Select one child to help you count all of the hands. Write *pizza* on the first column of your graph and color in the appropriate number of squares.

4. Repeat the activity using the rest of the cards.

5. See if you can come up with something that applies to no one in the class, such as liking an obscure vegetable. Use this for the last column on your graph.

6. Discuss the features of the graph. Ask the children to determine which comment included the most or least children in the class.

7. Now transfer your graph to a book by writing each similarity and its result on a sheet of paper. Sketch a simple picture of each item. For example, one page might read, "There are 19 children in our class who like pizza." Continue until you have added every similarity to a page. On the last page, write whatever you discovered that none of the children liked.

. . . .

Extension: Have a child help you count every student in the class. Use this total to do some addition/subtraction using the similarities you have already graphed.

flag summer triangle mother eyes planet leaf

triangle △   mother 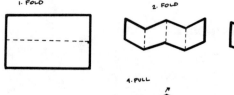   eyes   planet 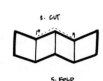   leaf 🍃

 (summer)

(flag)

(apple)

(me)

(snowflake)

(penny)

 (clock)

I Am! I Can! Booklet

Materials: copies of the "I Am! I Can!" pattern pages (pages 9–10), 12 x 18 pieces of construction paper, glue, crayons, scissors, tape measure, scale

1. Fold a piece of 12 x 18 construction paper in half lengthwise so you have one long folded strip of paper. Fold this in half and then in half again. Open the sheet fully and carefully make a slit down the middle of the page between the first and last folds, as shown. Refold the sheet in half lengthwise. Holding each end of the strip, slowly push the two ends together (the slit you made will begin to bulge) until they meet at the fold. Now fold all four "pages" together to make a book and crease the edges.

2. Have each child illustrate and complete the sentences (using phonetic spelling if necessary) in the "I Am! I Can!" pattern pages. Cut along the dotted lines and paste the pictures in your construction paper booklet.

1. FOLD   2. FOLD   3. CUT

4. PULL   5. FOLD

Self-Portrait

Materials: painting materials, paper

1. Give each child a piece of paper and have him or her paint a self-portrait. Mount the portrait on a larger sheet of construction paper to frame.

2. On a separate sheet of paper, have the children write or dictate five things that they think are unique or wonderful about themselves. Hang all of the portraits around the room and share the children's thoughts with the whole class.

Check for Understanding

- Each child should understand that he or she has characteristics that are similar to and different from other people's.
- Each child is a unique and special individual.

© McGraw-Hill Children's Publishing   8   0-7682-2810-7 *Learning Basic Vocabulary*

Name _____

1. I am! I can!
(A book about me!)

2. I am ____ inches tall.

3. I weigh ____ pounds.

4. _____ is my
favorite color.

0-7682-2810-7 *Learning Basic Vocabulary*

Name_____

I Am! I Can! Pattern Page

5. I like to eat
_____.

6. I am best at
_____.

**7. My favorite thing
to do is _____.**

**8. I am exactly how I am.
I can be anything I want
to be. I like me!**

0-7682-2810-7 *Learning Basic Vocabulary*

flag
summer
triangle △
mother
eyes
planet
leaf

My Body

Words to know: body, head, arm, hand, finger, leg, knee, foot, toe, elbow, hips, shoulders, chest

Overview: Our bodies have many different parts. Our bodies grow and change over time. All parts of our bodies are important.

My Body Changes

Materials: baby pictures, paper cutout of a small child or baby, paper cutout of a grown up, butcher paper, markers, and body parts flash cards

1. Before class, trace around the body of a small child (two to three years old) on a large sheet of butcher paper. On a second sheet of butcher paper, trace an adult.

2. Have each child bring in a baby picture from home.

3. Bring in a picture of yourself as a baby and as a kindergartner. Bring in a photo of one of your grandparents.

4. Talk about how everyone grows. Show the tracing of the small child. Talk about the small hands, feet, legs, etc. Talk about how the children were once this size, too.

5. Have the children show their baby pictures. Talk about how different the children look from when they were babies. Read *When I Was Little: A Four-Year-Old's Memoir of Her Youth,* by Jamie Lee Curtis (HarperTrophy, 1995). Make a list of the kinds of things the children did as babies (crawl, drink bottles, cry, etc.).

6. Show the picture of yourself as a baby, the picture when you were a child, and the picture of your grandparent. Talk about how everyone grows from being a baby.

7. Ask for a child volunteer who you can trace on a third sheet of paper. Tape this tracing next to the tracing of the baby. Compare. Have one child draw a body part flash card and point where that body part is on the baby and where that same body part is on a child. Notice how the two parts are still the same and in the same place, but different sizes. Make a list of the things the children have learned to do since they were babies or even since the beginning of the school year.

0-7682-2810-7 *Learning Basic Vocabulary*

triangle △   mother   eyes 👁👁   planet 🪐   leaf 🍂

8. Hang the third tracing of the adult. Have one child draw a body part flash card and point where that body part is on the adult and where that same body part is on a child. Notice how the two parts are still the same and in the same place, but different sizes. Compare the sizes of all three tracings.

Body Part Scramble

Materials: 3 body tracings from the "My Body Changes" activity, scissors, and body part flash cards

1. Take all three body part tracings from the previous activity. Cut the forms along the outside edges. Next, cut the bodies apart by separating the arms, head, hands, legs, and feet from the torsos.

2. Attach tape to the back of the body pieces and reassemble them at random into new body figures. For instance, put a baby-sized leg on the adult-sized torso. You can even put an arm where a leg should go. Tell the children that there's been a terrible accident—that you were carrying the body patterns when you slipped and fell. They got all mixed up.

3. Choose one child to draw a body part flash card out of a hat. Have him or her select that item and restore it to its proper torso. For instance, if "head" is drawn, the child removes one of the heads and returns it to its proper location.

Extension: Make three copies of the body parts flash cards. Cut out and separate the words. Have the children draw a word from a bowl and place the body part flash card in the appropriate place on one of the three body tracings.

Extension: Play another version of the body part scramble by placing all of the body part flash cards in a small paper sack. Draw two body parts out of the bag. The children then find a partner and match the two body parts. For instance, if you draw a "hand" and a "head," the children find a partner and put their hand on the head of their partner.

0-7682-2810-7 *Learning Basic Vocabulary*

 clock penny snowflake  me apple

flag

summer

Body Trace

Materials: scale, butcher paper, crayons, copies of body part flash cards, glue

1. Work with a partner to help you trace around your body.

2. Color your body pattern as desired. Make sure to include a face. See if you can make your body silhouette look just like you with the same clothes, the same color of hair and eyes, etc.

3. Take a sheet of the body parts flash cards and separate each word. Paste these words in the appropriate places on your body tracings.

Check for Understanding

- Do the children know the names of their body parts? Can they identify them?
- Do the children understand that their bodies change as they grow?

triangle △

mother

eyes

planet

leaf

0-7682-2810-7 *Learning Basic Vocabulary*

Healthy Me

Words to know: healthy

Overview: I can take care of myself to be healthy. Eating right, exercising, and getting enough sleep are things I can do to help my body grow strong and healthy. The things I do on the outside of my body help the things inside my body, too.

Inside Me

Materials: picture of a computer, camera, 2 balloons, plastic bag, straws, electrical wire, rubber bands, hammer, sponge, plastic wrap, coffee filter, 3 feet of plastic tubing, box, child-sized body tracing on a large sheet of craft paper, tape

1. Place the items listed above, except the paper and tape, in a large box.

2. Tape the craft paper body tracing securely to the wall or bulletin board.

3. Discuss the idea that the things we do to the outside of our bodies effect all of the things inside our bodies, such as muscles, bones, organs, and blood.

4. Have a child choose an item from the box. Talk about that item and how it is similar to a body part inside the children's bodies (see chart). Discuss what they can do to keep each body part healthy. As each part is discussed, attach it in the proper place to the body tracing.

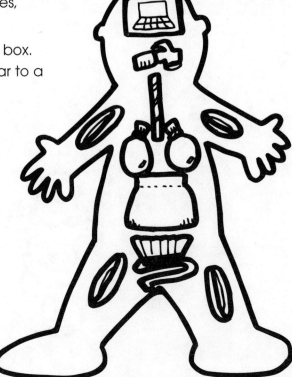

Item from Box	Body Part	Keeping Healthy
picture of a computer	brain	Our brain needs good food, and "brain exercise," thinking and learning every day, will keep our brains healthy.
camera	eyes	Our eyes make pictures for the brain to develop. Protecting our eyes from the sun and eating good foods will help keep our eyes healthy.
two balloons	lungs	Our lungs hold in the air we breathe, and then send it with our blood through the rest of the body. Eating good food, exercising, and avoiding harmful drugs will help our lungs work properly.
plastic bag	stomach	After we chew our food, the stomach collects the food until the body is ready to use it. Eating good foods will keep our stomachs healthy.
straws	blood vessels	Our veins and arteries carry blood through the body. Eating good food and getting a lot of exercise will help our bodies stay healthy.
electrical wire	nerves	We have nerves that run all through the body. They send messages back and forth to the brain. Eating right and getting a lot of sleep will help our nerves stay healthy.
rubber bands	muscles	Our muscles are like rubber bands. They expand and contract to move the body. Eating right and exercising help keep our muscles working right.
hammer	teeth	Our teeth are like tiny little hammers. They break up the food we eat. Eating good food, brushing, flossing, and seeing the dentist regularly will help keep our teeth healthy.
sponge	heart	Our hearts are muscles that act much like sponges. The blood comes in, and then the heart contracts (or squeezes) and sends the blood out of the arteries back into the body. Our heart needs good food and a lot of exercise to stay healthy.
coffee filter	kidneys/liver	Our kidneys and liver are special organs that help filter out all of the stuff our bodies can't use, sending it out of the body. Eating right and avoiding harmful drugs and alcohol will keep our organs healthy.
3 feet of plastic tubing	colon	Our colon takes all of the stuff we don't need inside our bodies and sends it out. Good food and exercise will keep our colons working right.
plastic wrap or rubber glove	skin	Our skin is like a big sheet of plastic wrap. It protects all of our insides by keeping them in, and it keeps out all of the things that shouldn't get into our skin. Eating right will help our skin stay healthy.

flag summer triangle mother eyes planet leaf

0-7682-2810-7 *Learning Basic Vocabulary*

 triangle △   mother   eyes   planet   leaf

My Body Needs ...

Materials: "My Body Needs" pattern pages (pages 17–19), scissors, crayons, stapler, glue, 3" pieces of string, fabric scraps, red construction paper

Make a copy of the "My Body Needs" pattern pages for each child. Separate along dotted lines, collate, and staple together. In addition to coloring each page, the children may add other collage articles to complete the picture as follows:

- Food and water (draw pictures of food or paste pictures of food from magazines)
- Clothes (color clothes on the body)
- Exercise (glue a piece of string in the child's hands for a jump rope)
- Plenty of sleep (cut a small swatch of fabric and glue it over the child for a blanket)
- A lot of love (cut a heart from red construction paper or draw one on the page)

Check for Understanding

The children understand that by eating right, getting enough sleep, exercising, and not putting harmful substances in their bodies they will stay healthy on the inside and outside.

0-7682-2810-7 *Learning Basic Vocabulary*

Name _____

My Body Needs Pattern Page

food and water

clothes

Name _____

My Body Needs Pattern Page

exercise

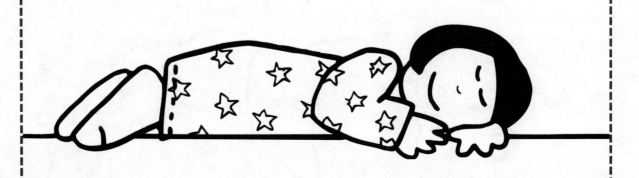

plenty of sleep

Name _____

lots of love

Nutrition

Words to know: food, vitamins, grains, breads, fruits, vegetables, meat and protein, dairy, fats and sweets

Overview: Food affects the way we feel physically and mentally. Food can be categorized into six basic food groups: grains and cereals, fruits, vegetables, meat and protein, dairy, and fats and sweets. We should eat balanced meals every day. We should eat fats and sweets sparingly.

I Am What I Eat

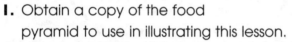

Materials: pictures of foods cut from magazines, paper plates, glue, food pyramid

1. Obtain a copy of the food pyramid to use in illustrating this lesson.

2. Food can be categorized into six basic food groups: grains and cereals, fruits, vegetables, meat and protein, dairy, and fats and sweets. We should eat balanced meals every day.

3. The grains and cereals food group consists of foods such as bread, pasta, muffins, oatmeal, and rice. These foods contain vitamin B, which helps digestion and makes healthy nerves, and carbohydrate, which give us energy. It is recommended that children eat 6 to 11 servings a day.

4. The fruit group includes apples, oranges, pears, bananas, and many more. These foods contain fiber, vitamin C (which helps muscles and gums), as well as many other vitamins and minerals. Two to four servings of fruits are recommended to keep you healthy and growing right.

5. The vegetable group includes potatoes, beans, lettuce, broccoli, and peas, to name a few. In addition to other vitamins and minerals, these foods contain vitamin A, which helps you fight infections and also improves your eyesight. Vegetables are also full of fiber, which helps your body digest the food you eat. Three to five servings of vegetables are recommended.

 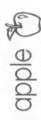

6. Proteins help build and repair muscles and other body tissues. Meat such as hamburger, chicken, pork, and fish, as well as foods such as nuts and eggs are included in this group. Two to three servings per day is all you need.

7. Foods that are included in the dairy group are milk, cheese, and yogurt. These contain vitamin D, which helps bones grow strong and keeps your teeth healthy. It is recommended that you have two to three servings per day.

8. Fats and sweets are foods you should eat only occasionally.

9. If you eat too many of any one group and not enough of another, your body can get sick or you can become unhealthy.

10. Read *Gregory, the Terrible Eater,* by Mitchell Sharmat (Scholastic, 1989), or *Bread and Jam for Frances,* by Russell Hoban (Harper and Row, 1964). Talk about making good food choices and eating a variety of foods to keep your body working just right.

11. Scatter the food pictures you have cut from magazines on the floor.

12. Write the food group words across the chalkboard or bulletin board, leaving space beneath each word to tape pictures of foods that fit into each category.

13. Have the children take turns choosing pictures and sorting them into the appropriate category. Tape these pictures to the board below their food group.

14. Next, divide the class into groups of three children. Give each child a paper plate. Each team of three chooses food pictures from the board that represent the total number of servings (6–11 grain, 2–4 fruits, 3–5 vegetables, 2–3 protein, and 2–3 milk). The team then divides the foods into three separate meals by taping the pictures on the paper plates.

15. Have each team share with the rest of the class the meals they prepared.

Sort and Eat

Materials: pictures of foods cut from magazines, paper plates, glue, food pyramid

Have the children create more healthy meals by choosing an appropriate balance of foods. They can paste the pictures to the paper plates.

Check for Understanding

Eating a balanced diet helps a person grow strong inside and outside the body.

flag summer triangle mother eyes planet leaf

summer · flag · apple · me · snowflake · penny · clock

Hygiene

Words to know: germs

Overview: Proper care of the body includes brushing and flossing teeth, washing hands, and observing general cleanliness. Germs can be found everywhere and cause illness. Most illness can be prevented.

Taking Care of Me

Materials: large sheet of butcher paper, markers

1. We must do many things to keep ourselves clean and healthy. Have the children list as many things as they can think of that humans do to keep clean. Ideas to begin with: bathe and shower, wash hands with soap after using the restroom, brush teeth, etc.

2. On a large sheet of butcher paper, sketch a copy of the man from the illustration in the poem "The Dirtiest Man in the World," from *Where the Sidewalk Ends,* by Shel Silverstein (Harper & Row Publishers, Inc., 1974).

3. Read the poem to the class.

4. Have the children recall the details of the poem as you add illustrations such as flowers growing out of the man's ears, and flies buzzing all around.

5. Reread the poem to see if the children forgot any details. Add these illustrations to your "Dirtiest Man in the World" and hang him near the sink to remind the students to wash their hands and use soap.

6. Discuss the physical and social consequences of the behavior exhibited by the "Dirtiest Man in the World." What would happen if we stopped bathing? What would happen if we stopped washing our clothing or if we didn't brush our teeth? Not only would people want to avoid us (much like the poem suggests), but our teeth would get cavities; we could get sick from using our dirty hands to put things in our mouth; our hair would be a tangled mess; and we would attract flies or maybe even a pig or two!

7. Make a checklist of things to do daily to keep our bodies clean and healthy.

Take Care Not to Share

Materials: sock, dried beans

1. Create a small beanbag by filling a sock with dried beans. Tie a knot in the top to seal the beans inside. You may want to decorate the sock to turn it into a "germ."

2. There are lots of things we like to share with our friends. Have children suggest items they like to share. List the items on the chalkboard.

3. There are also a lot of things we shouldn't share with our friends.

4. Show the children the beanbag "germ" you created. Let the children know that this is just a fun representation of a germ. Explain that real germs are microscopic (or very small) cells that invade our bodies and make us sick.

5. Have all of the children sit in a circle. Hand the "germ" beanbag to one child. Play a favorite song or some music while the children pass the beanbag around the circle. Periodically stop the music. When the music stops, the child who is holding the germ has just been "infected." That child must leave the circle, but he or she leaves the "germ" behind to be passed on by the other players.

6. Have all of the children return to the circle and explain how this game is much like how germs are passed from one person to another.

7. Pass along the following information to the children: Germs are everywhere. The best defense to avoid getting sick is to do those things that keep germs from getting inside your body. Part of keeping healthy requires being vigilant at hand washing, covering your nose and mouth when you sneeze or cough, not sharing food you are eating, and staying home when you're not feeling well.

8. Make a list of things not to share with friends. Reiterate the importance of following the "No Sharing" rules to keep everyone in the class healthy.

flag
summer
triangle
mother
eyes
planet
leaf

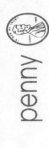

Healthy Me Booklet

Materials: "Healthy Me Booklet" pattern pages (pages 25–26), scissors, crayons, stapler, glue, 1" strips of yarn or other "hairlike" material, soap shavings, toothpaste, facial tissues cut in fourths

Make a copy of the "Healthy Me Booklet" for each child. Have students color the pages as desired. Paste a soap shaving on page 2. Paste the yarn strips on top of the heads on page 3. Paste a small piece of facial tissue in the child's hand on page 4. Rub a little toothpaste across the toothbrush on page 5. Staple the pages together.

Check for Understanding

- Bathing or showering and using soap help keep us clean.
- Staying clean helps us stay healthy.
- Germs are found everywhere, and they can make us sick.

Name _____

Healthy Me Booklet Pattern Page

I. Healthy Me!

2. I wash my hands.

3. I comb my hair.

0-7682-2810-7 *Learning Basic Vocabulary*

Healthy Me Booklet Pattern Page

4. I look for germs that might be there.

5. I brush my teeth.

I cover my nose. I take care of me, and boy it shows!

Five Senses

Words to know: sight, smell, taste, touch, hearing

Overview: Our five senses help us explore the world. We can use our five senses to discover and explore the world around us.

Five Senses Food

Materials: bacon, electric frying pan or hot plate, napkins

When you talk about food, the obvious senses you think of are taste and smell. But there are many different foods for which you can use all five senses to explore.

1. Choose a food in which you can use all five senses to observe and explore. Some suggestions might be popcorn, bacon, flavored potato chips, and carbonated drinks.

2. Talk about how the children can use all five senses to explore the food they eat. Hold up a package of bacon. Ask the children how they know it is bacon. (They can tell by their eyes because it looks like bacon.) Have the children help you compose a list of descriptive words that describe bacon by sight.

3. Remove a piece of bacon from the package and allow the children to feel the bacon. What does it feel like? Add a list of descriptive words that describe the bacon by feel. (Take a short break so students can wash their hands thoroughly with soap.)

4. Place the bacon in a warm frying pan and ask students to listen. What sounds do they hear as the bacon is cooking? Add the listening descriptive words to your list.

5. As the bacon begins to cook, you will be able to smell the bacon. Ask the children what kinds of words they can use to describe the smell of frying bacon.

6. After you have cooked the bacon and it has cooled, give each child a piece. Ask if the words the children would use to describe the bacon after it is cooked are different from the words they used before the bacon was cooked.

7. Finally, have everyone taste the bacon. Ask the children what words you would use to describe bacon. Add these to your list. Also have the children consider the sound of the bacon as it crunches in their mouth. Add all of these descriptive words to your list and review all of the ways the senses help the children explore the world around them.

flag · summer · triangle · mother · eyes · planet · leaf

triangle △   mother   eyes 👁 👁   planet 🪐   leaf 🍂

See It, Hear It, Smell It

Materials: pictures of objects clipped from magazines that we use our senses to identify, large box

1. Hold up one picture. Have the children classify the picture as depicting something they can see, hear, taste, touch, or feel. Some of the pictures you choose may have more than one option for sensory exploration.

2. If desired, make a "Five Senses" book by collating and binding the pictures.

Sensory Exploration—Feely Boxes

Materials: medium-sized box with a circle cut out of the side large enough for a hand to pass through, variety of textured objects stored in a brown paper bag

1. Have a partner turn his or her back while you place an item from the paper bag to the box. Be sure to seal the bag so your partner cannot see the items left inside the bag.

2. Place the item in the box and close the lid.

3. Have your partner reach inside the box through the hole and describe the object to you by how it feels. See if your partner can guess what the object is.

Smell Detectives

Materials: several empty yogurt containers with lids, cotton balls

1. Punch several holes in the lids of yogurt containers. Saturate cotton balls with a variety of extracts or perfumes, place a different cotton ball in each container, and replace the lid.

2. With each child working with a partner ask them to figure out what each container holds. A fun alternative is to place several related smells (i.e., gingerbread, peppermint, cinnamon, pine, etc.) in the containers and see if the children can classify the smells as a group.

Left margin (top to bottom): summer , flag , apple , me , snowflake  , penny 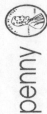 , clock

 clock  penny snowflake me apple

Taster's Table

Materials: plastic spoons; prepared vanilla pudding; variety of extracts such as peppermint, lemon, and strawberry; food coloring; paper plates

1. Place one teaspoon of extract in a cup of prepared vanilla pudding to make flavored pudding. Stir thoroughly. Add food coloring if desired. Avoid coloring the pudding a color that the children would expect for that flavor. For instance, color the lemon-flavored pudding pink.

2. Place a small dollop of each pudding flavor on a paper plate and let each child taste the pudding to see if he or she can determine the flavor by taste.

The Eyes Have It

Materials: variety of optical wear including prescription glasses, sunglasses, glasses with amber or other colored lenses, binoculars, 3-D glasses, and magnifying glass; variety of pictures: big print, small print, colored, black and white, and monochrome; mirror

1. Before using the different optical-enhancing glasses to view a variety of different pictures, predict what you think you will see or how your vision will be altered with each optical wear. Talk about it with a partner.

2. Take turns using the different lenses. Share your observations of the effects of each type of eyewear with your partner. Does he or she agree with your assessment?

3. Take turns viewing yourself in the mirror with the different glasses. Do you look different in any of them? Are you bigger, smaller, or changed in any way when you look at yourself through the glasses?

Check for Understanding

• We have five senses: sight, hearing, taste, touch, and smell. They are all important in helping us explore the world.

• We can make observations about the world by using our five senses.

flag
summer
triangle
mother
eyes
planet
leaf

summer flag apple me snowflake penny clock

Emotions

Words to know: emotions, happy, sad, angry, frightened, surprised, proud

Overview: Emotions are a reflection of the feelings we have inside. We express our emotions through facial expressions and body posture. Our emotions influence our actions.

If a Picture's Worth 1,000 Words ...

Materials: pictures cut from magazines or newspapers depicting people in emotional situations, emotions flash cards

1. An old saying expresses that a picture is worth 1,000 words. Ask if anyone can guess what this means. After the children have had a chance to respond, explain that even though pictures do not usually have words on them, they often tell a story. We can use words to describe what is happening in a picture, what might have just happened, and what might be about to happen, all based on the clues we get from the picture.

2. Choose a picture such as from a birthday party. Most likely everyone in the picture is happy. Find the emotions flash card word *happy* and tape it to the picture. Ask the children how they think the children in the picture are feeling. Is anyone not happy?

3. Talk about what is happening in the picture. Next, talk about what may have happened right before the picture was taken. Finally, talk about what might happen next.

4. Repeat with the other pictures, labeling each picture.

5. Next, show a picture of a face without any context clues. Talk about how that person is feeling based on the emotion showing on his or her face. Label the face with the appropriate emotions flash-card word.

6. Discuss how we have emotions because of something we are experiencing. We all have ways of reacting to the emotions we are feeling.

Emotions Charades

Material: emotions words flash cards, film or digital camera

1. Talk about how everyone feels emotions. Some people show their emotions quite plainly on their faces. Others are more stoic. Sometimes they show their emotions with their whole bodies, too.

2. Have one child draw an emotions word flash card from a hat. Have that child act out that emotion with only their face.

3. Take a picture of the child displaying that emotion. Save or download the pictures for an independent practice activity later.

4. Have the rest of the class see if they can guess the emotion the child is showing. If necessary, have the child add a few context clues with body language to help the class accurately guess the emotion.

Extension: Sing "If You're Happy and You Know It," including as many of the different emotions as possible. Make a list of commonplace experiences that your children are familiar with, such as getting exactly what they want for their birthday or learning to tie their shoes. Have the children show you on their faces what they would be feeling during each experience.

Emotions Sequencing

Materials: "Emotions Sequencing" pattern pages (pages 32–33), crayons, scissors, glue, construction paper

1. Make a copy of the "Emotions Sequencing" pattern pages for each child.

2. Have the children color, cut out, and reorder each set of pictures to tell a story.

3. Paste the pictures in order on a sheet of construction paper. Have the children relate the story the pictures are telling, including the emotion being shown.

Check for Understanding

- We have many different emotions.
- Our emotions influence our actions and reactions.

Name_____

Emotions Sequencing Pattern Page

Name _____

Emotions Sequencing Pattern Page

triangle mother eyes  planet leaf

My Family

Words to know: family, mom, dad, sister, brother, grandparent

Overview: Families come in a variety of sizes and combinations of family members. Every family is unique. Families change over time.

Family Show and Tell

Materials: craft sticks, 7 tin cans each labeled separately with one of the following the words—*Mom, Dad, Brother, Sister, Grandparent, Cousin, Aunt,* and *Uncle*

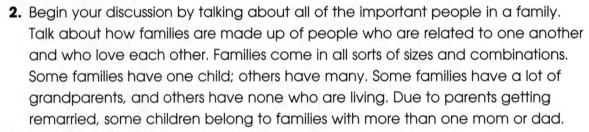

1. Solicit the following information from the children's families: Who is a part of the child's family (this could include family members such as cousins, aunts/uncles, and other family members who do not live in the household), and what is this person's relationship to the child in your class? Have each child bring in a picture of his or her family to share.

2. Begin your discussion by talking about all of the important people in a family. Talk about how families are made up of people who are related to one another and who love each other. Families come in all sorts of sizes and combinations. Some families have one child; others have many. Some families have a lot of grandparents, and others have none who are living. Due to parents getting remarried, some children belong to families with more than one mom or dad.

3. Have the children take turns sharing their family pictures.

4. Next, begin by talking about mothers (write *mother* on the board) and the kinds of things mothers do. Make a list on the chalkboard. Have each child place a craft stick in the can labeled "Mom" to represent his or her mom. (Be sure to include stepparents as needed.)

5. Repeat with the other family members.

6. Count the total number of sticks in each can and compare the tallies from all of the cans. Which can had the most? Are there more parents than grandparents? Why or why not?

Left margin: summer, flag, apple, me, snowflake, penny, clock

© McGraw-Hill Children's Publishing

0-7682-2810-7 *Learning Basic Vocabulary*

 clock penny snowflake me apple

Families Change

Materials: large map of the world; small, round, solid-colored stickers; two pictures of a family before and after someone has been added to or lost from the family through birth, death, divorce, or marriage

Find out from each student's parent(s) if his or her family has ever lived in another town or city.

1. Talk about how all families change.

2. We all grow and change. Babies are born. Siblings move out. Family members sometimes pass away unexpectedly. The activities we choose change to reflect the different interests of our growing bodies. Have the children share experiences where their families changed because of an addition or a loss of a family member.

3. Our spaces change. Sometimes we move to a new house. Sometimes we trade rooms or spaces inside our existing house. Due to an employment change or remarriage, moving is sometimes inevitable. On a large map of the world, use small stickers to pinpoint the areas the children have lived in. Discuss the map and how far some children have traveled to their new home.

4. Sometimes grown-ups change. Sometimes Mom or Dad move away to a new home. Sometimes Mom or Dad gets remarried and a whole new part of a family is added. Sometimes parents change jobs, or start working when they had been a stay-at-home parent.

5. All of these things are changes that affect families. Sometimes the change is easy to handle, and sometimes the change is hard. It is common to be curious and even a little worried about changes. Help the children know that in all of these examples, changes occur because of the natural course of events. Remind them of the important people in their lives they can talk with when they are feeling anxious about a recent or impending change.

© McGraw-Hill Children's Publishing

0-7682-2810-7 *Learning Basic Vocabulary*

 summer
 flag
 apple
 me
 snowflake
 penny
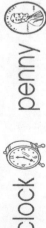 clock

Family Portraits

Materials: copy of the "Family Portrait" pattern page (page 37), markers or crayons

1. Make one copy of the "Family Portrait" pattern page for each child. Have the children draw a picture of their family. Help them label the members.

2. Use the space provided at the bottom of the frame to write or dictate something about the children's family. Some suggested prompts: "My favorite thing to do with my family …" "I love my family because …" and "My family helps me to …"

Funny Families

Materials: magazines, scissors, glue, white paper, 9 x 12 pieces of colored construction paper

1. Have the children sort through the magazines in search of pictures of people. Carefully cut around the bodies to remove them from the magazine pages.

2. Once you have collected all of the pictures, arrange them on a sheet of paper to create a funny family portrait, as though the people had posed together to be photographed.

3. Mount the portrait collage on a sheet of colored construction paper and display it in the room.

Check for Understanding

- Families come in all sizes and a variety of combinations.
- Families change and that change affects each family member.

Name _____

Family Portrait Pattern Page

summer

flag

apple

me

snowflake

penny

clock

Staying Safe at Home and in the Car

Words to know: safety, seatbelt

Overview: We can do many things to keep ourselves safe. It is important to know which products or objects have harmful effects and to know basic rules of safety at home and in the car.

Safety Tips

Materials: colored paper cut into star shapes, markers

1. Being safe means being careful to follow rules, being aware, and using all of your senses to keep out of harm's way. Sometimes harmful things happen. But all of us can do things to prevent accidents and keep ourselves safe.

2. Read *Officer Buckle and Gloria,* by Peggy Rathmann (G.P. Putnam's Sons, 1995). Talk about the safety tips discussed in the story.

3. Have each child suggest a safety tip for the class to observe. On the paper stars, write *Safety Tip #1* followed by the first tip given. Have the child offering the suggestion illustrate the safety tip.

4. Read all of the safety tips aloud and display them in a prominent location.

Stop and Think

Materials: stop sign; props such as household cleaners and matches, to help prompt discussion in the safety scenarios activity (optional)

1. Obtain a stop sign from the school safety patrol officer or create your own.

2. Play "Stop & Go" by having all of the children stand at one end of the classroom or playground. Select one child to be the safety patrol person. This child stands at the opposite end of the classroom or playground. When the safety patrol child lowers the stop sign, the children move quickly (without running) across the playing area. At any time, the safety patrol child raises the stop sign, at which time everyone must immediately stop in place. Anyone who continues to move must go back to the beginning point and start over. Play continues until one child reaches the safety patrol person. They switch places and play begins again, this time by moving across the room or playground in a different way, such as walking like a duck, walking backward, etc.

3. Talk about how important it is to STOP and THINK when it comes to being safe.

clock penny snowflake  me apple

Good For You/Bad for You

Materials: "Good For 'You'" pattern page (page 40), red dot stickers, crayons

1. Write *stop* on several red dot stickers. You will need at least five stickers per child.

2. Make a copy of the "Good for You" pattern page for each child. Have the children color the pages as desired.

3. Place a "stop" sticker on each picture that depicts a child who is being unsafe.

Home Scavenger Hunt

Make a copy of the following checklist of safe things for the children to hunt for at home with their families:

- 2 outlet covers
- 1 stop sign
- someone wearing a seatbelt in your own car and in another car
- 1 flashlight
- 2 things that are hot
- 5 things you should never put in your mouth
- something that makes you feel safe
- 1 smoke detector

Check for Understanding

- We can do many things to keep ourselves safe.
- The children have a basic knowledge of safety rules.

Name _____

Good for "You" Pattern Page

0-7682-2810-7 *Learning Basic Vocabulary*

Personal Safety and Strangers

Words to know: safety, strangers

Overview: It is important to learn to recognize our surroundings—areas of safety, danger, and risk. We should establish boundaries and know that it is OK to say no when someone is doing something we don't feel comfortable about.

S-A-F-E

Materials: 4 pieces of construction paper, each with one letter (S-A-F-E) printed on it, pictures of a variety of people, chalk

1. Personal safety is the way we keep ourselves safe.

2. Place the "S" poster on the board.

3. *S* stands for **Stranger.** What is a stranger? A stranger is someone you don't know. Not all strangers are bad, but not all strangers are good either.

4. How do you know a stranger is good or bad? You can't tell just by looking. The best rule is to stay away from strangers. Read *Never Talk to Strangers,* by Irma Joyce, (Golden Books, 1991). Reinforce the following concepts about strangers:

   - You shouldn't take the time to talk to a stranger. If the stranger asks for directions, it's OK to say you don't know (even if you do). If the stranger asks for help finding something, such as a lost pet, tell the person you need to ask your parent first.

   - It isn't rude to walk away from a stranger. If a stranger tries to take you with him or her scream as loud as you can, "THIS IS NOT MY PARENT!"

   - Never open the door to let someone in your house.

   - Never tell someone on the phone that your parent is not at home.

5. Place the "A" poster on the board.

6. *A* stands for **Always.** Always tell a trusted grown-up when you are hurt, scared, or confused—especially when you told someone no, but he or she did something to you when you anyway. If something doesn't seem right, trust your instincts and get help. Even when someone tells you not to—always tell someone you trust.

triangle △   mother   eyes 👁👁   planet 🪐   leaf 🍂

7. Place the "F" poster on the board.

8. *F* stands for **Fences.** It's important to establish boundaries. Fences are barriers. They keep in what you want in, and they keep out what you want out. Play this quick and simple game to illustrate: Draw a small circle on the ground with chalk or make a small circle with masking tape. Have one child stand inside the circle. Have another child stand outside the circle. Tell the child in the circle that his or her job is to catch the child on the outside of the circle and to tag that person. The problem is that the child inside the circle can't go past the line, the imaginary fence. It won't take long before the children see that the boundaries keep the first child away from the second.

9. We can establish personal "fences" (the kind you can't even see) for our own comfort and safety. If someone is touching you or talking to you in a way that is hurtful, makes you feel uncomfortable, or you just don't like, you can set up your "fences" by telling them to stop. Practice saying "No!" like you mean it. If that doesn't work, remember the letter *A*. Always tell a trusted grown-up.

10. Place the "E" poster on the board.

11. *E* stands for **Eyes** and **Ears.** When you get lost, use your eyes and ears to help you find your adult. Call out for help and then stop and listen with your ears to help you locate your parent or guardian.

12. If you need help or get lost in a store, use your eyes to look for someone who works at the store or look for another mom with kids to help you. Never leave the building without your parent.

13. If you are going to be in a big crowded space, use your eyes and ears to establish a safe meeting place. Go directly to that spot if you get lost. Don't wander around looking for your parent.

14. Always take a buddy with you. Always check in.

Stranger Face

Materials: facial features cut from magazines, paper, glue

1. Place all of the eyes in one container, ears in another, noses in a third, mouths in another, and hair in yet another.

2. Have the children draw a circle for a face.

3. Create a stranger's face by gluing the assorted features to the face.

4. Have the children write "I can be safe!" at the bottom of their picture.

Check for Understanding

• The children can reiterate rules of personal safety.

Emergencies

Words to know: emergency

Overview: It is important to know home phone numbers, address, full name of parent or guardian, and emergency phone numbers. This information as well as other safe thinking skills helps us know what to do in emergencies.

What Is an Emergency?

Materials: 2 telephones

1. To be as safe as you can be, you should know some basic information as well as what to do in an emergency.

2. What is an emergency? An emergency is when something happens that needs immediate attention. Fires and serious injuries are two examples of emergencies. What other emergencies can you think of? List the ideas on the board.

3. Talk about the differences between a minor and a major emergency.

4. Talk about the differences between a real emergency and something we want or need right away. When the curtains catch on fire, that is an emergency. Wanting a snack after school is not an emergency. Make a list of emergencies and nonemergencies. Read the list. Have the children shout "911" if it is a real emergency and "Ho-Hum" if it is not.

5. Here are some important rules to remember about emergencies:

   • Stay calm. Practice taking a deep breath. Focus and ask yourself if this is something you can do or if you need help.

   • Find a big person for help.

   • Call 911 if you need fire, police, or medical attention. When you call 911 or your local emergency dispatch, a person will ask for some information:

      a) What is wrong, what kind of help do you need

      b) Your name or your parent's name

      c) Your address and phone number

6. Practice dialing the emergency operator.

flag summer triangle mother eyes planet leaf

triangle △   mother 👩   eyes 👁 👁   planet 🪐   leaf 🍂

summer flag apple me snowflake penny clock

Phone Number Scramble

Materials: 3 x 5 cards, 4" x 30" strips of paper, marker

I. Write one number on each of the cards, 0–9. Make sure you have a big enough assortment of numbers for each child to collect all of the numbers in his or her phone number, plus a few extra of each number.

2. Write all of the children's phone numbers (in large print) on strips of paper.

3. Scatter the 3 x 5 number cards around the floor in the middle of the room, number side up.

4. Let the children, a few at a time, walk to the middle of the room and take one number in their phone number. Tell them to return to their place with the card and place it in sequence on their phone number strip.

5. The children can continue scrambling for numbers until everyone has completed his or her phone number.

I Know!

Materials: "I Know" pattern page (page 45), crayons, pencils

I. Make a copy of the "I Know" pattern page for each child.

2. Have the children practice their home phone number, address, and parent's name.

3. Have them color and fill in the appropriate information in the space provided.

4. Award stickers, ribbons, or other incentives when the information is mastered.

Check for Understanding

- Does each child know what to do in an emergency?

- Does each child know his or her home phone number, parents' names, and address?

0-7682-2810-7 *Learning Basic Vocabulary*

Name_____

I Know Pattern Page

phone number

address

parent's name

emergency 911

0-7682-2810-7 *Learning Basic Vocabulary*

triangle △　mother 　eyes 👁👁　planet 🪐　leaf 🍂

summer

flag

apple

me

snowflake

penny

clock

My Community

Words to know: community

Overview: Each of us is a member of a community. Many different people live and work in a community. A community has buildings, homes, and people who live in the area.

Community Circles

Materials: large sheet of paper, markers

1. Talk about communities and how a community is made up of many different people who work and live together. A community consists of homes where people live, parks and other areas where people play, and businesses where people work. When you are a member of a community, you fit into a unique set of groups, or smaller environments, within the community.

2. Draw a big circle on the sheet of paper. This circle represents all of the places and people in a community (see illustration).

3. Draw a small circle in the middle of the large circle. This circle represents each child.

4. Have the children think of all of the groups that they are a part of in their community—groups that are bigger than just them, but not as big as the whole community. (Family, school, sports teams, church, and clubs are all examples of smaller circles.) Draw Venn diagrams to represent each of these groups.

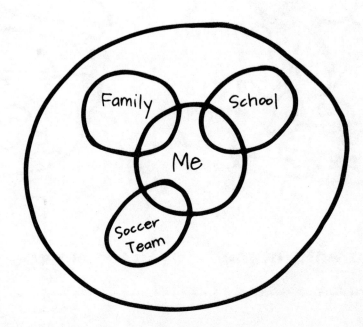

0-7682-2810-7 *Learning Basic Vocabulary*

Map My Community

Materials: large sheet of butcher paper, community word flash cards, "My Community" pattern pages (pages 49–53), glue, scissors, crayons

Make a copy of the "My Community" pattern pages. Duplicate the house pattern so you have enough for each child. Have the children color their house and cut it out. Color and cut out the other community buildings.

1. On a large sheet of butcher paper, draw and label the streets around your community.

2. Talk about how your community is tied together by the people, the places they work, and the roads that get people from place to place. On the large map you have created, show the children the location of the school. Paste the picture of the school in place. Tape the community word flash card above the school. Talk about how the school is a place where teachers come to work (and children come to learn) in order to make the community a better place. Ask the children for the name of their street and pinpoint it on your map.

3. Have the children suggest other places of business that contribute to the community.

4. Finally, have the children paste their house on the map in a location where they would like to live. Have them consider different areas of the community and the pros and cons of living in each area. For instance, they may wish to put their home next to the fire station because it would be quick and easy for the firefighters to respond to an emergency at their house, but it would also be noisy with the fire trucks coming and going, sirens blaring, etc.

5. Consider other aspects of the community: Is it good to have all of the houses close together? Should the houses be close to the stores? Are there other buildings or businesses the children know of that have not yet been included in your community? Have the children draw in these buildings.

triangle △   mother   eyes 👁 👁   planet 🪐   leaf 🍂

 summer

 flag

 apple

 me

 snowflake

 penny

 clock

My Community Map

Materials: copy of the "My Community" pattern pages (pages 49–53), crayons, scissors, glue, 6 x 18 strips of construction paper

1. Using the pattern pages, have the children color and cut out each building. Paste the buildings as desired on a 6 x 12 strip of paper to make a street in your community.

2. Let each child give the "street" on his or her paper a name.

3. Have the children add pictures of living and nonliving things around their community (people, animals, trees, cars, and stop signs).

4. Have the children write or dictate a short description of what is happening on their street.

Check for Understanding

• I am part of a community and many smaller groups within that community.

• A community includes the people who live and work together.

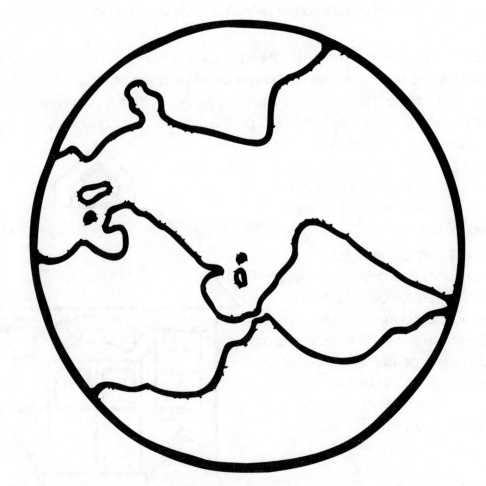

Name _____

My Community Pattern Page

post office

store

Name _____

My Community Pattern Page

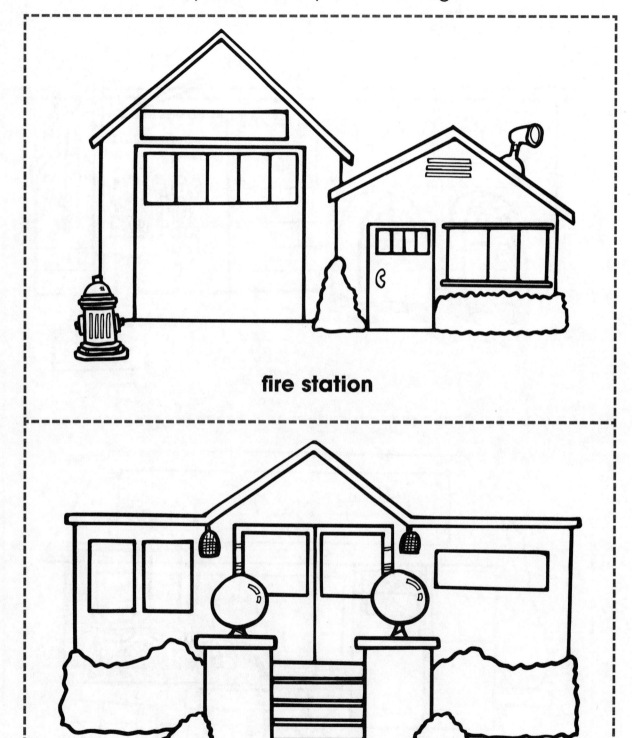

fire station

police station

Name _____

My Community Pattern Page

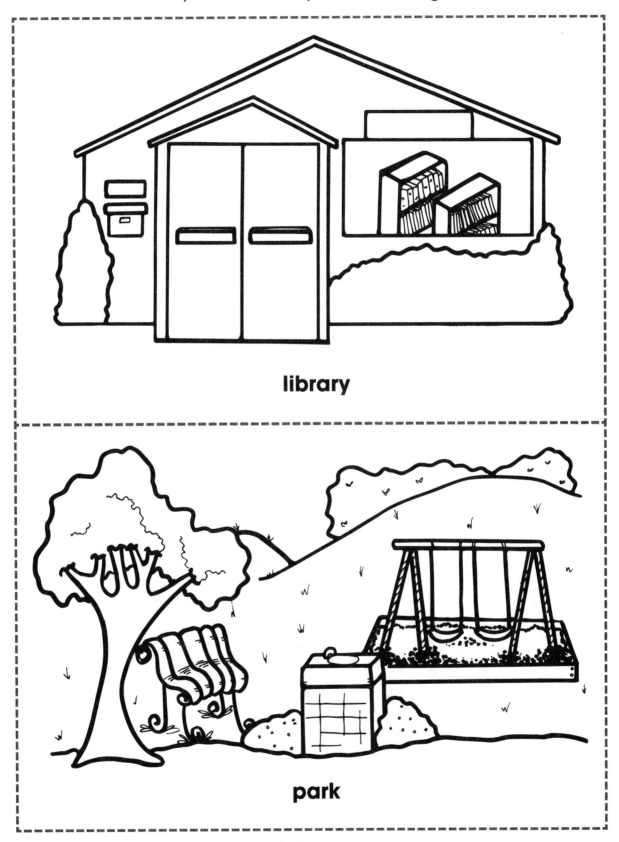

library

park

Name_____

My Community Pattern Page

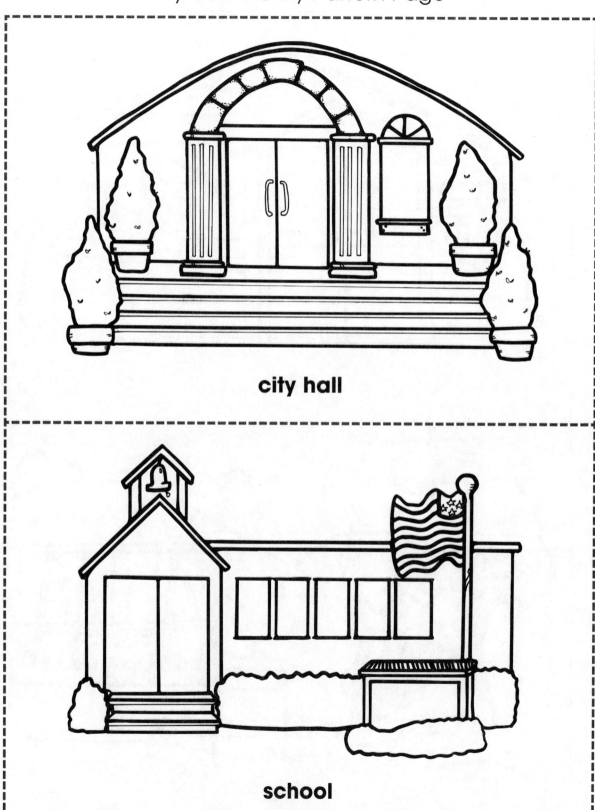

city hall

school

Name _____

My Community Pattern Page

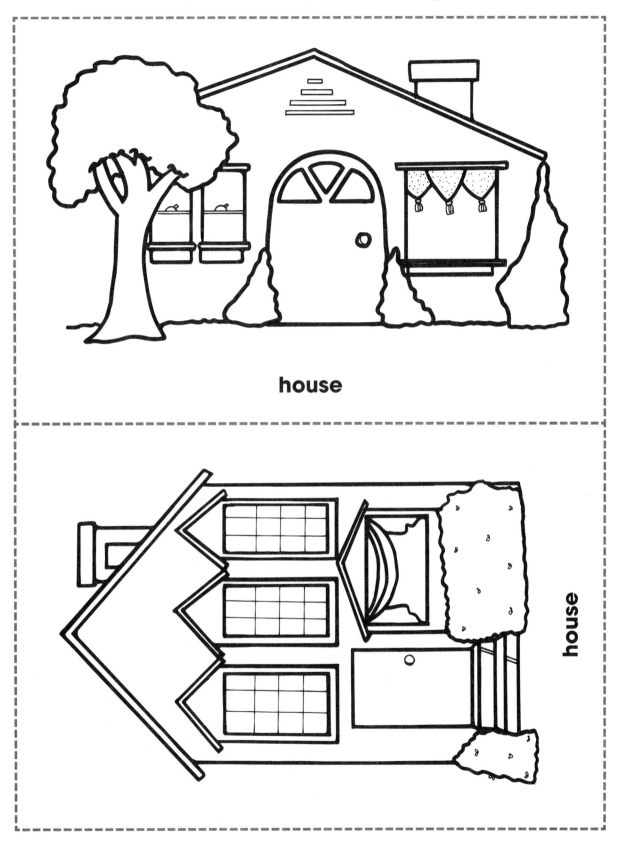

house

house

triangle △   mother   eyes   planet   leaf

summer

Community Helpers

Words to know: community helpers, police officer, firefighter, postal worker, nurse, doctor, mayor

Overview: There are many workers in a community. Everyone works together to make a community.

Who Am I?

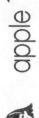
flag

apple

me

Materials: assortment of tools or hats associated with different occupations, large box, prepared community helper question cards (described below)

1. Collect an assortment of tools and hats that are associated with different occupations. Include representations of community helpers such as doctor, police, and firefighter as well as other individuals in the community who contribute to the children's lives. Place all of the items in a box. Selected items might be hats or pieces of uniforms, tools, or other objects associated with each job.

2. Prepare a community helper question card for each occupation represented. Write basic information about each worker in question format. For example, one card might read, "I drive a truck and deliver letters to homes. Who am I?"

3. Talk about the purpose of community helpers. Why do we need so many people to help keep our communities running smoothly?

4. Invite a parent or another adult who works in the community to come to class and share how they are part of the community.

5. Have a child choose one of the community helper question cards and read the contents to the class. Have that child see if he or she can select one item from the box that corresponds to the description on the card.

snowflake

penny

clock

0-7682-2810-7 *Learning Basic Vocabulary*

clock   penny   snowflake   me   apple

flag

summer

triangle

mother

eyes

planet

leaf

Extension: Discuss the importance of each group or person's role in the community. For instance, what would happen if no one wanted to be mayor? What would happen if no one wanted to live in the community? Discuss your own classroom community and the importance of everyone doing his or her part to work together. Write a letter to a helper in your community thanking the person for his or her contribution to the community. Arrange for an excursion to one of the many places in your community.

When I Grow Up

Materials: copy of the "When I Grow Up" pattern page (page 56), crayons

1. Make a copy of the "When I Grow Up" pattern page for each child.
2. Have the children illustrate what they would like to be when they grow up.
3. On the paper, have the children write or dictate their thoughts as well as a list of the things they believe the career they have chosen entails.
4. Have each child share his or her ideas with the rest of the class. Or bind the pages together to create your own classroom of community helpers book.

Check for Understanding

- Many workers are needed to keep a community running smoothly.

When I Grow Up Pattern Page

clock  penny snowflake me apple

Money

Words to know: penny, nickel, dime, quarter, work

Overview: People work to earn money for things they want and need. Pennies, nickels, dimes, and quarters are all different coins with different values.

1—2—3 Change

Materials: an assortment of real coins (one set for each child), money word flash cards

1. Talk about the different coins that we use. Give each child a set of coins to examine. Compare the sizes, colors, textures, and other distinguishing features of each coin.

2. Compare values. Place a penny on the ground. Place the appropriate money word flash card next to the coin. Place a second penny next to the first penny to represent the value of that coin. Each penny equals one cent. Count the pennies. Have the children find the penny in their collection and place it on the ground in front of them.

3. Place a nickel on the ground below the penny. Place the appropriate money word flash card next to the coin. Have the children find the nickel in their collection and place it on the ground in front of them. Next to the nickel, line up five pennies. One nickel equals five cents. Count the pennies.

4. Do the same activity using the dime and quarter.

5. Compare all of the coins and their values.

6. Line up two nickels and the number of pennies that equal the coins. Count the total value of the nickels and compare it to the value of the dime. Repeat with the other coins.

Extension: Use an assortment of coins for patterning practice. For example, make an AB pattern with nickels and pennies. Or create an ABB pattern with quarters and pennies.

Shopping Spree!

Materials: several copies of the quarter funny money on the "Funny Money/Piggy Bank" pattern page (page 60), stickers, pencils, assortment of colored and patterned papers

1. Copy the funny money on colored paper, laminate, and cut out.

2. Create a "Pencil Store." Have a small table with a box of pencils. Create a sign that says "Pencils, $.25" Do the same setting up a "Paper Store" and a "Sticker Store."

3. Discuss how adults work to earn money for the things they want and need. Ask the children to list the kinds of things people spend their money on. Remind the class that before people can spend money, they need to earn it. Arrange for a class project, such as cleaning up the playground, to earn "money" for the activity.

4. Give each child six funny money quarters.

5. Practice "buying" things so the children are familiar with the value of the funny money. If they buy one pencil, they must forfeit one quarter.

6. Each child must purchase one sheet of paper. The children can then decide if they want to spend the rest of their money on pencils, stickers, paper, or any combination until they run out of money.

7. Let the shopping begin: Choose one child to be the shopkeeper at each table. Have the children use their money to make their purchases.

8. After the children have spent all of the money, have them return to the group and discuss the things they bought.

summer　flag　apple　me　snowflake　penny　clock

clock penny  snowflake me apple

flag

summer

triangle △

mother

eyes

planet

leaf

Piggy Pennies

Materials: "Funny Money/Piggy Bank" pattern page (page 60), pennies, snack-sized resealable plastic bags

1. Make a copy of the piggy bank and penny pattern cards on the "Funny Money/Piggy Bank" pattern page. Separate the piggy bank and the penny pattern cards on the dotted lines. Color the piggy bank. Tape or staple the plastic bag to the back of the piggy bank.

2. Have one child draw two penny pattern cards. Place the penny pattern cards on the piggy bank where indicated by the dotted boxes. Have the child match the number of pennies on the penny pattern cards by placing pennies on the table below the piggy bank.

3. Count the number of pennies in each box and add them together to get the total number of pennies. Repeat several times using different combinations of penny pattern cards. When you are done, store the cards in the bag.

Extension: Create an opportunity for dramatic play by setting up a classroom store with plenty of play money for purchasing items and making change.

Check for Understanding

- Coins have different values.
- People work for money to buy things they want and need.

Name _____

Funny Money/Piggy Bank Pattern Page

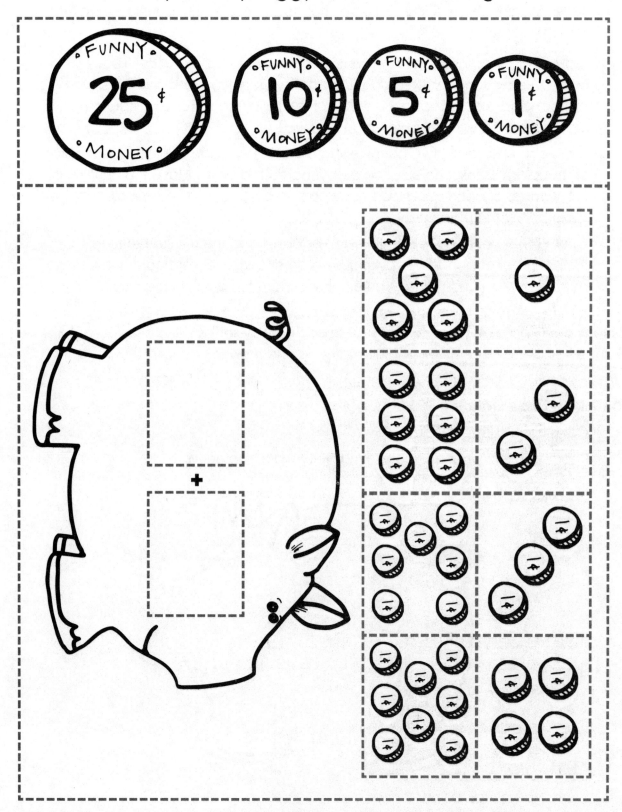

0-7682-2810-7 *Learning Basic Vocabulary*

clock penny snowflake me apple

flag

My Country

Words to know: country, flag, freedom

Overview: The United States of America is where many people live. Many symbols remind us of our country and our freedom. Many individuals have made significant contributions to U.S. history.

Where Do You Live?

Materials: globe or map

1. Locate the United States on a map or globe. What countries are its neighbors? How does it compare in size with the other countries?

2. Locate your state on the map or globe. Which states border your state? Have you ever lived in another state?

3. Locate your city in your state. Is your city big or little? Can you find the surrounding cities or communities?

4. Draw a Venn diagram to represent how a city is part of a state and a state is part of the country. Continue by showing how the country is a part of the world.

Symbols of Freedom

Materials: "Symbols of Freedom" pattern page (page 64), tape measure

1. Show each symbol from the "Symbols of Freedom" pattern page as you discuss it. For more information about our country and the symbols of freedom, see *http://bensguide.gpo.gov*.

2. Declaration of Independence. On July 4, 1776, the Declaration of Independence, a paper declaring the United States as a free nation, was signed. In part, the Declaration states that all men are free and equal, that we each have the right to live free and do those things that bring us happiness. It also states that we can choose a government to make the laws (or rules) we will live by. Talk about what rights everyone in the class has.

3. Liberty Bell. The Liberty Bell is in Philadelphia, Pennsylvania. It was rung to announce the signing of the Declaration of Independence. When you have great news to announce, what do you do?

4. Bald eagle. The bald eagle is a bird found in North America. Why do you think the bald eagle was chosen as a national symbol of freedom?

5. Statue of Liberty. The Statue of Liberty was given to the United States by the French government. The statue is 150 feet high and welcomes all of the people coming into the New York Harbor. How high is 150 feet? In a large open area, measure 150 feet, placing children as markers for every 10 feet.

summer triangle mother eyes planet leaf

6. Flag. Our flag has 13 red and white stripes with a blue field in the upper left-hand corner filled with white stars. Each star represents one of the 50 states in the union. Compare the current flag with those of the past. Compare the flags of other countries. How are these flags similar and different?

7. Because the people who founded America felt so strongly about freedom, we have opportunities to make decisions for ourselves that children from other countries may not. Every four years adults have the opportunity to vote for the President of the United States and other men and women who help make the laws and rules that we live by.

8. Take a simple class vote. Have the children vote which story they want read to them. Talk about how even though we may disagree, the most votes decides what the class will do.

9. As a class, write a letter to the President, a senator, or your local representative to Congress, thanking him or her for making the laws that keep everyone free.

Important Contributions

Materials: pictures of famous U.S. statesmen and women

1. A statesman is someone who makes a contribution to his or her country through words or actions.

2. Choose a few names to research from the following list. Find pictures and write down each person's contribution and story in a few simple sentences. Share the stories with the class and place the picture and stories on the bulletin board.

Great U.S. Statesmen and Women: Pocahontas, George Washington, Booker T. Washington, Daniel Boone, Benjamin Franklin, George Rogers Clark, Mercy Otis Warren, Dolly Madison, Harriet Tubman, Abraham Lincoln, Martin Luther King, Jr.

Extension: Find out about the different symbols for your own state. What does the flag look like? How is it similar or different from the flag of the United States?

 clock penny  snowflake me apple

 flag

What Will You Do?

Materials: paper, markers, construction paper

1. Have the children draw a self-portrait on a sheet of paper.

2. On a separate sheet of construction paper, have them write or dictate what they think their contribution will be. What stories will people tell about them? Will they be honest? Will they help others?

3. Staple the pictures and thoughts to the bulletin board along with the pictures and stories of famous U.S. historical figures.

summer

My Flag

Materials: crayons, construction paper, dowels or balloon sticks, scissors

1. Have the children decorate their own flag by coloring a piece of construction paper. Encourage them to think about using symbols on their flags—pictures and objects to represent them and things that are important to them. They may want to include items from of the "Symbols of Freedom" pattern page (page 64).

2. Tape the flags to a dowel or long stick. Have a parade through the classroom to show off your flag.

triangle

mother

Check for Understanding

- We live in the United States of America.

- Our national symbols help to remind us of our freedoms.

- Many people have made great contributions and sacrifices for the freedoms of this land.

- We can contribute to this great country by being good citizens.

eyes

planet

leaf

© McGraw-Hill Children's Publishing

0-7682-2810-7 *Learning Basic Vocabulary*

Name_____

Symbols of Freedom Pattern Page

flag

summer

triangle ▽

mother

eyes

planet

leaf

School People and Places

Words to know: kindergarten, school, teacher, principal, librarian, office, library, gym, cafeteria

Overview: School is a community of students, teachers, and others who work together to create an atmosphere for learning. Respect, cooperation, and consideration are needed for a school to be a good place to work and learn.

School Scavenger Hunt

Materials: camera, copy of the "School Bus" pattern page (page 68), large sheet of craft paper, school map, stickers, pencils

1. Take pictures of teachers and other officials at school, such as the principal, the school secretary, the cafeteria supervisor, the nurse, the librarian, the custodian, teachers, and teachers' assistants. Cut around the figures in the photos to remove the background. Label each photograph with the person's name and position at the school. Copy the photos on card stock and cut out each figure so you have one of each person for each child.

2. Write the name of your school on the side of the bus pattern and make a copy for each child. Glue around the outside edges (sides and bottom only) of the bus and paste it to another sheet of card stock. When the glue has dried, cut around the outside edges of the bus to create a pocket envelope.

3. Make a copy of a map of your school. Place a star on each of the places (office, library, gym, playground, etc.) that you will be visiting on your scavenger hunt. Include all areas of the school that the children need to be familiar with. Copy this on the back of the School Scavenger Hunt Checklist (page 69).

4. Make a copy of your school map on a large sheet of craft paper.

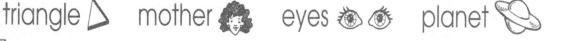

triangle △ mother eyes planet leaf

 summer
 flag
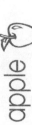 apple
 me
 snowflake
 penny
 clock

5. For your school scavenger hunt, arrange in advance for a short visit to each of the other staff members. Give them the copies of the cut-out photographs to give to the children on their visit.

6. Discuss how many people are needed to keep a school running smoothly. Talk about all of the different people in your school and the jobs they do. Be sure to include yourself in this discussion. Talk about what would happen if one of the staff chose not to show up or do his or her part. What would happen if the custodian stopped cleaning?

7. Ask the children to take a look at the large map you have drawn. Have a child locate the classroom. Take turns finding the locations of other important places such as the playground, the office, and the cafeteria.

8. Give each child a copy of the bus pocket envelope and the map/scavenger checklist. Show how the map is just like the map in your classroom. Have the children locate on their map the different places in the school.

9. Tell the children to turn the paper over and look at the items on the school scavenger hunt checklist. Discuss each item and tell the children that they will be looking for each item as you move about the school today.

10. As a class, go on a mini field trip. Remind the children to look for the things on their scavenger hunt checklist. Take the bus envelopes and follow your maps as you begin in the office. Have each staff member share his or her responsibilities and give each child the picture that you took. Have the children put the picture in their bus pocket. Place a sticker on the office on the map.

11. Continue through the school until you have met all of the staff members, collected their pictures, and marked their spaces on your map.

12. When you return to the classroom have the children remove the pictures from their bus and lay them on the floor in front of them. Have the children see if they can find the picture of the principal, can recall the principal's name, and state one thing the principal does. Find the office on the map and tape a picture of the principal in the office. Continue with the other staff members.

0-7682-2810-7 *Learning Basic Vocabulary*

clock  penny snowflake me apple

Kissing Hand

Materials: crayons, paper, washable ink, potato or lip print stamp

1. Cut a large potato in half. On the raw edge, draw the shape of lips and cut away to create a lip print potato stamp.

2. Have the children trace around their hand with a crayon on a piece of paper. Ask them to color the rest of the page as desired.

3. Using the lip stamp and ink, make at least one lip print on the palm of the child's traced hand.

4. On the bottom of the page, have the children write or dictate their thoughts about what they love and miss about their parent while they are at school.

My School Bus

Materials: crayons, craft sticks

1. Color all of the pictures of the staff and the school bus.

2. Have the children make a small self-portrait. Cut out the drawing.

3. Secure all of the photos to craft sticks and use the pictured puppets in a puppet show to role-play the first day of school, a time when the children had to visit the school nurse, etc.

Check for Understanding

- The children know that coming to kindergarten is a big step, one to be proud of.
- The children know the different places around school and the people who have responsibilities in their school.

Name_____

School Bus Pattern Page

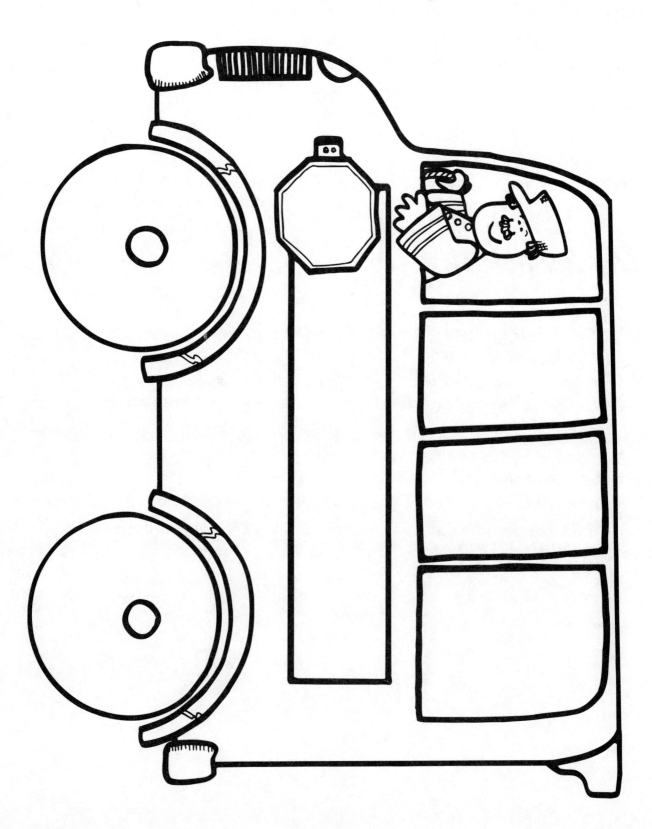

Name _____

School Scavenger Hunt Checklist

summer
flag
apple
me
snowflake
penny
clock

School Rules and Friends

Words to know: rules, friends

Overview: We have specific rules in our classroom, and each person is responsible for his or her own actions and behavior. There are consequences for our choices. Individuals within a community must follow rules, accept responsibilities, share ideas, cooperate, negotiate to solve problems, and make their own decisions.

Our Classroom Community

Materials: 3 x 5 cards, pictures of class members, resealable plastic bags

1. Gather a picture of each child in your class or take pictures a few days before this activity. Have the photos processed in time to present this lesson.

2. Send home a note before this lesson, requesting that the children bring something to share all of their classroom friends. Suggestions might be stickers, feathers, golf tees, etc.

3. So we can have a good day at school, we all need to cooperate. Ask the children what would happen if you, as the teacher, decided to be ugly to everyone and disobey the rules? Everyone must work together to create a good learning environment.

4. On 3 x 5 cards, write the letters of the alphabet or numbers (each letter or number on its own card).

5. Give each child a letter card. Have him or her, in turn, place the letter in the proper alphabetical order. Sing or say the alphabet as you point to each letter. Repeat the activity, setting one letter aside so that when you sing or say the alphabet, you know which letter is missing.

clock    penny   snowflake   me   apple

6. A classroom is just like this activity. Everyone must work together to make it complete.

7. In our classroom community, there are things we do as a group and on our own. This includes following rules, accepting responsibilities, sharing ideas, cooperating with one another, and negotiating to solve disagreements or problems.

8. Lay out the photos of the children in rows on the floor so that the children can see all of the pictures. Point out each picture and have the child in the photo stand and wave.

9. Have all of the children close their eyes and remove one of the pictures. Have the children open their eyes to see if they can figure out which picture is missing. Return the photo and play again.

10. We are all a part of an important class community. We work together, we play together, we learn together, and we are friends. Read *Making Friends,* by Fred Rogers (Puffin, 1996). Talk about what it means to be a friend. Reinforce that every child in the class is a friend.

11. Have the children distribute the items they brought to share with their friends. Encourage them to tell why they chose the item they did. Encourage the children to say "thank you" and "you're welcome" as the tokens are being passed out. Place the items in a resealable plastic bag.

School Rules

Materials: "Classroom Rules" pattern pages (pages 73–74), markers, tape

1. Enlarge the pattern pages of the classroom rules so one rule is on each page. Color and laminate.

2. Using the classroom rules you just enlarged (be sure to include your own personalized rules for your classroom), talk about each rule and why it is important.

3. Tape all of the classroom rules facedown on the board in random order. Have the class play concentration, trying to find the matching classroom rules. Once a child finds a match, have him or her tell the importance of the rule and the consequences for breaking the rule.

summer

flag

apple

me

snowflake

penny

clock

Friendship Collage

Materials: construction paper, glue, crayons

1. Empty the contents of the resealable plastic bag containing the items shared in the classroom community activity on pages 70–71.

2. Have the children explore the contents. Which item is their favorite? Do they remember who brought each item? Sort the contents and group them by color, shape, size, and texture. Count the items. Make sets of one, two, three, four, and five items.

3. Next, glue each item on the construction paper as desired. Add color and details.

Cooperation Mural

Materials: paper, crayons or markers, scissors, large sheet of craft paper that covers the entire length of a wall

1. Have each child draw a picture of himself or herself and cut out the figure.

2. Hang a large sheet of craft paper along one wall. Have the children work together to create a classroom mural. Cooperate to decide what the mural will be about. Have the children add the pictures of themselves and draw any other additions (animals, objects, etc.) to the mural as desired.

Check for Understanding

- The children know and understand the classroom rules and consequences for not obeying rules.

- Rules are important for us to work together as a classroom community.

- Friends come in all sizes, shapes, and personalities. Friends are people who care about one another.

Name _____

Classroom Rules Pattern Page

1. We are respectful with our words. We always use "please," "thank you," and "you're welcome."

2. We are respectful with our words. We do not use ugly words.

3. We are respectful of our teacher. We always follow the teacher's directions.

4. We are respectful of our environment. We clean up after ourselves.

Name_____

Classroom Rules Pattern Page

5. We are respectful of one another. We are all friends.

6. We are respectful of one another. We do not hurt others.

7. We are respectful of one another. We share and take turns.

8. We are respectful of one another. We stay seated, listen, and participate at group time.

0-7682-2810-7 *Learning Basic Vocabulary*

flag

summer

triangle

mother

eyes

planet

leaf

Color My World

Words to know: colors, red, yellow, blue, green, purple, orange, black, brown, white

Overview: This lesson will help refresh the children's memories of colors. Through repetition and a variety of activities, the color words will be introduced and reinforced.

Color Walk

Materials: camera, notebook, glue

1. Familiarize your children with the basic colors by reading *Brown Bear, Brown Bear, What Do You See?* by Bill Martin (Henry Holt & Co., 1983). Take the class for an outdoor "color walk." As you walk, have the children take turns pointing out colored objects. You might even chant the children's names as they take turns finding colors, such as, "Anna, Anna, what do you see?" Anna would then report, "I see a yellow sun looking at me!" Or call out a color and see if each child can find a different object of that color.

2. Use a camera during your walk to take a picture of each color found. Create a class color book by pasting the pictures in a small notebook, listing each color word on a separate page. Share the book in class the following day. See how many of the colors the children can recall from the previous day's walk by asking, "Who remembers what we found on our walk that was yellow?" Have the children help you list other objects of each color on the color pages in your book.

summer

flag

apple

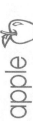
me

snowflake

penny

clock

Color Cats

Materials: "Skat the Cat" pattern page (page 77), color word flash cards, markers, crayons

1. Make a copy of the "Skat the Cat" pattern page on colored paper so that you have one of each color: black, blue, brown, green, orange, purple, red, white, and yellow. Write the appropriate color word on each colored cat. Laminate the cats for durability. You will find corresponding color word flash cards at the back of this book.

2. Before beginning the chant, spread the color cats out across the floor and have the children take turns matching the color word flash cards to the colored cats. Next, stack the cats face up in a pile and hold them so the fronts of the cats are facing forward. Stroke the colored cat as you all chant:

Skat, the cat, was happy and fat.
If you don't like his color, he will change it like THAT!

At this point, pull the cat from the front of the pile and place it behind the others. Have the children take turns calling out the color of the new cat as it is revealed. Repeat the activity having the children take turns matching the appropriate color word flash card with the colored cat.

Color Race

Materials: paper bag, color word flash cards, die

1. Place all of the color word flash cards in a paper bag. Choose one child to draw a card from the bag. Choose a second child to roll a die. These two children then become a team. They must find the number (the number rolled on the die) of objects that are the color that matches the color card drawn. For a little added excitement, use a timer and give each team one minute to collect all of the items.

2. Once a team has collected the items, have the class compare the items and discuss ways they are similar and different. Are all red objects always the same color red?

Name_____

Skat the Cat Pattern Page

77 0-7682-2810-7 *Learning Basic Vocabulary*

Color Families

Words to know: primary, red, yellow, blue, orange, green, purple

Overview: Colors are divided into different color families. The primary colors are red, yellow, and blue. Mixing the primary colors creates all of the other colors.

Rainbow in a Jar

Materials: large bucket, towel for cleanup, water, 6 clear glass containers, food coloring, paper plate, markers, color word flash cards

Colors come in "families," or groups. There are two basic color families—primary and secondary. Primary means "first." By mixing the primary colors (red, blue, and yellow) in different combinations, you can make the secondary colors (purple, green, and orange) and many more variations.

1. Divide a paper plate into six wedges (as shown).

2. Fill one clear glass container with water. Put several drops of blue food coloring in the jar to create blue water. Watch the blue food coloring as it dissipates in the clear water. Talk about how the water is "grabbing up," or absorbing and mixing, to create totally blue water. Label the jar with the color word *blue*.

3. Color one wedge of the paper plate blue. Label the wedge "blue."

4. Create yellow water and label the jar. Leave the wedge next to blue uncolored and color the next wedge yellow. Label the wedge. Repeat the activity creating red water and coloring a red wedge as illustrated.

5. Ask the children: "What will happen if I mix blue water and yellow water together?"

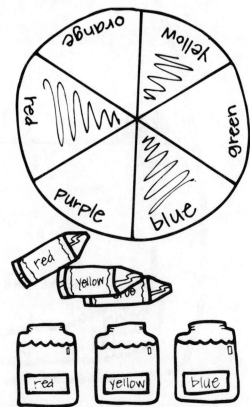

clock  penny snowflake me apple

6. Pour a little blue water and a little yellow water into an empty jar to create a new color of water: green. Yellow, blue, and green are a color family. On the paper plate, color the wedge between the yellow and blue wedges green.

7. Repeat with the other combinations (use the bucket for discarded water) until you have created purple and orange water. Color in the appropriate wedges on your plate.

8. Read *Little Blue and Little Yellow,* by Leo Lionni (HarperTrophy, 1995). Talk about what happens when Little Blue gets mixed with Little Yellow.

9. Experiment by mixing other combinations and volumes of water.

10. Talk about the color wheel you have created. Have the children point out the primary colors—or the colors you used to create all of the other colors. Have the children make other observations about the color wheel, the color families, and the colored-water experimenting you have done.

Color Mixing Partner Parade

Materials: music, musical instruments, color card necklaces (see instructions below), string, color card flash cards

1. Create color card necklaces by laminating colored paper (red, yellow, green, blue, orange, and purple). Cut the paper sheets into sixths. Label each color card with the appropriate color word. Punch a hole in the center of one end of the card. Lace with a piece of string that is long enough to create a color card necklace. Make one per child, but twice as many of the primary colors.

2. Have all of the children stand in a circle. Give each child a color card necklace so that there are twice as many blue, red, and yellow necklaces as purple, orange, and green.

3. Play some marching music and have the children march around the room.

4. Tell them when the music stops, everyone should freeze in place. Stop the music. Then tap two children who are wearing primary color cards. These two partners greet one another with a handshake and then make a color family by finding another child who is wearing a card that completes the family. For instance, if you tap a child wearing a blue color card and a child wearing a red color card, they must complete the color family by finding a child who is wearing a purple color card. Let the children make as many families as possible. The families parade around the room, elbows linked, until the music stops again.

0-7682-2810-7 *Learning Basic Vocabulary*

flag

summer

triangle

mother

eyes

planet

leaf

summer

flag

What Happens If ... Egg Carton Colors

Materials: foam egg cartons; bucket and towels for cleanup; jars of red, yellow, and blue colored water (labeled with the color words); eye droppers; paper plates divided into 6 pie wedges

1. Demonstrate the use of the eye droppers and caution about mixing colors in the jars of water.

2. Following the "Rainbow in a Jar" activity, have the children create their own colored water combinations by placing drops of colored water in the egg carton slots, then coloring a wedge on the color wheel.

3. Continue adding drops and coloring until the color wheel is completely filled in, as demonstrated previously in the group activity.

4. If time allows, let the children experiment creating new colors by adding different amounts and combinations of colored water.

apple

Check for Understanding

- Red, yellow, and blue are primary colors.

- Primary colors can be mixed to create new colors—red and blue: purple; yellow and blue: green; red and yellow: orange.

me

Other great color books to include in your color family curriculum:

A Color of His Own by Leo Lionni (Dragonfly, 1997)

Mouse Paint by Ellen Stoll Walsh (Voyager Books, 1995)

How Is a Crayon Made? by Oz Charles (Prentice Hall, 1988)

My Crayons Talk by Patricia Hubbard (Henry Holt & Co., 1999)

Purple, Green and Yellow by Robert Munsch (Annick Press, 1992)

snowflake

penny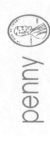

clock

clock    penny    snowflake    me   apple

Shapes

Words to know: circle, triangle, square, rectangle, cube, cone, cylinder, sphere

Overview: Circles, triangles, squares, and rectangles are the basic shapes. Sphere, cone, cube, and cylinder are the geometric forms of these shapes. We can recognize shapes in the environment and use them to describe objects. Shapes can be combined to create other objects.

Shape Detectives

Materials: shape word flash cards

1. There are four basic shapes: circles, squares, triangles, and rectangles. These basic shapes, alone and combined, make up most of the objects we see around us.

2. Read *So Many Circles, So Many Squares,* by Tana Hoban (Greenwillow, 1998), or *Circles, Triangles, and Squares,* by Tana Hoban (Simon and Schuster, 1974). As you look at the pictures in the book, have the children point out the shapes they see. Some shapes are obvious and easy to see.

3. We can find basic shapes in our environment. Select one child to be the first shape detective. Hand the child one of the shape word flash cards and send him or her on a hunt around the room for something that matches the shape on the card. Once the child finds a matching item, have him or her return with the item (if possible) to the group. After all of the children have had a chance to be shape detectives, ask them to help you sort the shapes into groups.

4. When we make shapes into three-dimensional objects, squares become cubes, triangles become cones, rectangles become cylinders, and circles become spheres. Read *Cubes, Cones, Cylinders, & Spheres,* by Tana Hoban, (Greenwillow 2000). Play shape detectives again, this time using the geometric shape word flash cards.

5. Take the class on a shape walk to find other shapes in the children's environment. Take a checklist with you and write down the examples of each shape and its geometric counterpart that you find. Review your list when you return to the classroom.

6. Send a note to parents or guardians encouraging them to help the children find an example of each shape at home.

flag
summer
triangle
mother
eyes
planet
leaf

summer
flag
apple
me
snowflake
penny
clock

Shape Story

Materials: shapes colored, cut out, and laminated from the "Shape Story" pattern (page 83); a copy of the "School Bus" pattern page (page 68) colored, cut out, and laminated. Read the story, (pages 85–86) maneuvering the shapes as described in the story. After finishing the story, let the children suggest other ways the shapes could play together to create new things.

Extension: Look for objects in your classroom that are a combination of two or more shapes.

Food Snack Shapes

Materials: assortment of shaped snack foods, sandwich-sized resealable plastic bags, "Snack Sort" pattern page (page 84), pencil

1. Gather an assortment of shaped snack foods such as crackers, cheese, or sandwich meat cut into shapes; grapes; raisins; popcorn; and carrot sticks. Place a handful of snack shapes into a sandwich bag—one for each child.

2. Make a copy of the "Snack Sort" pattern page for each child.

3. Using the pattern page, have the children remove the contents of their snack bag one at a time and sort them into shape categories. Once all of the shapes are sorted, have the children count each shape group and tally the total number of snack pieces of each shape on the snack sheet in the shape provided. Ask the children to draw the number of shapes equal to the total number of snack pieces inside the space provided. For instance, if eight snacks were circular, the children should write *8* inside the circle provided and then draw eight circles in the space provided for circles. Repeat for all four shapes.

4. Next, have the children sequence each shape of snack food from smallest to biggest and then eat them in order.

Check for Understanding

- There are four basic shapes: circle, rectangle, triangle, and square.
- The children can recognize each shape, draw it, and create other objects from it.

Name_____

Shape Story Pattern Page

Name_____

Snack Sort Pattern Page

0-7682-2810-7 *Learning Basic Vocabulary*

clock    penny   snowflake    me   apple

Shape Story

It was time for Shape School to start. The circles were busy getting their school clothes in order. The squares spent their time school shopping. Triangles were just returning from a late summer vacation. The rectangles were rehearsing all of the things they needed to know for the start of kindergarten.

When they were in preschool, all of the circles were in Miss Sphere's class. *(Place the circles and the sphere on the board.)* They enjoyed playing "Ring Around the Rosy" and eating muffins for their snack. Their favorite thing to do was to roll to the top of grassy hill and then roll all the way to the bottom. *(Slide a circle down the board.)* Every once in a while one of the circles would hit a bump and come bouncing down the hill. But after a few tense moments, and big hugs from Miss Sphere, everything was OK again. The circles rolled for more circle fun. *(Roll the circles off the board.)*

Across the hall from the circles was Mr. Cube. He planned great lessons for the little squares in his class. *(Place Mr. Cube and all of the squares on the board.)* Their favorite game to play was four-square. And they always did square dancing on rainy days. Besides looking at books and playing with blocks, the squares loved snack time, especially square crackers and cheese cubes. The little squares loved to stack themselves up *(Stack four little squares up to make one big square.)* to look just like Mr. Cube. He always pretended not to recognize them when they did. *(Remove the squares and cube from the board.)*

The triangles' classroom was in the corner of the school. Mrs. Cone was their teacher. She was often frustrated by the little triangles' antics. *(Put the triangles and the cone on the board.)* Whenever she tried to get them to sit in a straight line, they wanted to sit all bunched up, making star shapes or pentagons. *(Make stars and a pentagon out of the triangles.)* Triangles loved to slide, often trying to slide down one another. *(Slide the triangles off one another.)* This gave Mrs. Cone great headaches. She was often found muttering, "You're giving me a gray hair," under her breath. The triangles loved sandwich day for lunch. Mrs. Bean, the cook, always cut the sandwiches into triangles. *(Remove the triangles and cone from the board.)*

The rectangles' classroom was next to the principal's office. Their teacher, Mr. Cylinder, was new, and the principal wanted the class to be close just in case Mr. Cylinder needed an extra hand. *(Place the cylinder and the rectangles on the board.)* Some of the rectangles were obedient but others were a little mischievous and occasionally tried to lie down during story time. *(Turn the rectangles on their sides.)* The rectangles loved playing basketball, tennis, and football because the playing fields felt so familiar. Their favorite snack was graham crackers. Mr. Cylinder had to dry up the rectangles' tears if one of the crackers accidentally broke. *(Remove the rectangles and cylinder.)*

triangle   mother   eyes   planet   leaf

 summer

 flag

 apple

 me

 snowflake

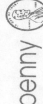 penny

 clock

Since all of the shapes enjoyed different things (*Place all of the circles in one corner, the squares in another, the triangles in a third, and the rectangles in yet another.*), the circles never played with the squares and often wondered why they seemed so odd. The rectangles were fairly sure that they were best. The squares thought the triangles looked funny. And the triangles were so busy playing tricks on Mrs. Cone that they didn't seem to notice or care that anyone else attended school.

This year all of the shapes were mixed up in one kindergarten class. Their new teacher, Ms. Oval (*Place Ms. Oval on the board.*), arranged a seating chart where all of the shapes were sorted at tables. (*Place one of each shape in a square pattern.*) But since the shapes didn't know one another, they rarely talked. They never played together at recess.

On the second day of school, Ms. Oval announced that there would be a school field trip. "Hooray!" all of the little shapes cheered. They loaded onto a bus. (*Place the bus on the board and put all of the shapes in the bus.*) All of the circles sat up front. The rectangles kept getting confused and sat backward on the bus until Ms. Oval straightened them out. The squares sat perfectly still in their seats. And the triangles were singing silly songs in the back.

Everything was going fine until "the big oops!" It happened when the bus driver was looking in the rearview mirror at the triangles instead of the road. He bumped into a curb. He swerved left and then right. Then he skidded to a stop. The little shapes came tumbling out of their seats into a big mixed-up pile. (*Pour all of the shapes out of the bus into a mixed-up pile.*)

Everyone was surprised. They didn't know what to do. Fortunately, everyone was just fine, although several of the shapes seemed stuck together. One of the circles was sitting on top of an upside-down triangle. (*Place the circle on top of the triangle.*) All of the other little shapes began to laugh and point. Together the circle and the triangle had made an ice cream cone. A rectangle found itself on top of two circles. (*Place the rectangle on top of two circles.*) Everyone clapped, because they looked like a wagon. Another triangle was perched on top of a square. (*Place the triangle on top of the square.*) They looked just like a house.

For the first time, the shapes realized how much fun cooperating and playing together could be. All of the little shapes spent the rest of the afternoon playing together, making new objects.

0-7682-2810-7 *Learning Basic Vocabulary*

clock penny snowflake me apple

Numbers

Words to know: numbers, one, two, three, four, five, six, seven, eight, nine, ten

Overview: Numbers are symbols we use to quantify objects. We can use numbers to count, to help us know how many, and to order things.

Number Bag

Materials: number word flash cards, 2 paper bags, "Action" word strips (see below)

1. Create action word strips by writing action words on small slips of paper. Make one action word for each child in class. Fold the strips in half and place in the paper bag.

2. Fold the number word flash cards in half and place them in the second bag.

3. Ask one child at a time to choose a number from the number bag and an action word from the other bag. Have the student do the action named on the action word strip the number of times listed on the number word flash card.

4. Discard the action word strip, but return the number card to the number bag. Have the first child choose the next player, and so on.

First, Second, Third

Materials: numerals 1–20 each written in large print on separate sheets of construction paper, number word flash cards

1. Tape the number pages in scrambled order on the board. Use the number word flash cards to label the number pages with the corresponding number word.

2. Tell the children that the numbers on the board are scrambled.

3. Select the children to participate by asking numbered answers such as "I'm looking for someone who has 10 grommets on their shoes."

4. Have the first child find the number 1 and place it on the left-hand side of the board. Continue the counting questions and number sorting until the children have put all of the numbers in order.

summer

flag

apple

me

snowflake

penny

clock

5. Give each child a numbered card. Have him or her search for an item in the room that can be combined into a set equal to the number on the card.

6. Have the children reorder the number cards, along with the objects they have collected.

Count and Write

Materials: "Count and Write" pattern page (page 89), assortment of collage materials (dried beans, beads, stickers, paper clips), glue

1. Copy the "Count and Write" pattern page on heavy card stock, one for each child.

2. Have the children glue on the number of objects indicated in each box. For instance, in the "5—five" box, the children would glue five small objects.

3. Next, count the objects and rewrite the number in the box provided.

Check for Understanding

• The children understand that numbers are symbols that represent a quantity of something.

• The children know how to order numbers.

Name_____

Count and Write Pattern Page

0-7682-2810-7 *Learning Basic Vocabulary*

My Day/Time

Words to know: hour, minute, second, morning, afternoon, evening, today, yesterday, tomorrow

Overview: Time is quantified in seconds, minutes, and hours. There is an order to each day's activities.

It's Time

Materials: poster board, time word flash cards, word strips, towel (for cleanup), props for routine sequencing (see list below)

1. Use the word strips to write down a list of the children's daily routines.

2. Write the words *morning, afternoon,* and *evening* on the board. Tape the word strips of the day's activities under the appropriate time of day.

3. Talk about how there is an order to each day's activities. Certain activities occur at certain times. You definitely wouldn't want to go to bed at 3 p.m., but that is a perfectly reasonable time for school to end.

4. Gather props (or pictures) for the sequencing sets below. Place three props for each sequence in a bag. As you remove the contents of each bag, have the children tell you the sequence of the three activities. You will want to have a towel handy and be perfectly willing to pour the milk on the floor if the child helping with the sequencing forgets to ask for the bowl first.

5. Suggested sequencing sets (you may add as many as you like):
   - Brushing Teeth: Toothbrush, toothpaste
   - Eating Breakfast: Cereal bowl, cereal, milk

6. Having a routine or an order that is logical is important. If you ate breakfast before you got out of bed, you might find waffles in your sheets. If you played before you got your homework done, you might not finish your homework.

0-7682-2810-7 *Learning Basic Vocabulary*

flag

summer

triangle

mother

eyes

planet

leaf

What Time Is It?

Materials: clock with second hand, stopwatch, word strips

1. Prepare a copy of the clock from the "Clockwork" pattern page (page 93), or provide a clock on which you can manipulate the hands manually.

2. Show the different features of the clock. Talk about how as time passes, the hands move around the face of the clock. The second hand takes 60 seconds to make one complete revolution. The minute hand takes 60 minutes to make one complete revolution. The hour hand takes 12 hours to make one complete revolution, and it goes around twice in one day.

3. Talk about the differences between a second, a minute, and an hour. What can you do in a second? (clap, kick a ball, etc.) What can you do in a minute, or in an hour? Talk about whether the ideas expressed are reasonable.

4. Use the stopwatch to time the actions.

5. Read *The Grouchy Ladybug,* by Eric Carle (Harper Trophy, 1996). Talk about the sequence of events in the ladybug's day.

6. Discuss how most of the events happen at specific times. School starts at ____ o'clock. Lunch is at ____. (Insert the appropriate times for your school schedule.) Bedtime is around 8:30. Make a list of different events during the day. Include activities that have a specific starting time, such as a sports game or practice, piano lessons, other after-school activities, church, movies, etc.

7. Talk about how we have specific times for events to keep order in our day and in the community. If we all have different ideas about when four o'clock is, we'd show up for the afternoon movie at the wrong time.

Extension: Talk about the differences between day and night. Read *Somewhere in the World Right Now,* by Stacey Schuett (Dragonfly, 1997). Talk about how even though it is daytime where you are, somewhere else in the world it is night.

Clockwork

Materials: "Clockwork" pattern page (page 93), metal brad, crayons, scissors, glue

1. Make a copy of the "Clockwork" pattern page for each child.
2. Have the children color the clock and the icons depicting times of day.
3. Cut out the clock's hands. Attach them to the face of the clock at the small dot with a brad.
4. Cut out each of the time of day icons along the dotted lines.
5. Look at the time of day in the first square below the clock. Now, find the icon that matches that time of day. Paste it in the space provided. Move the clock's hands to the four o'clock position.
6. Repeat with the other icons.

Sequencing My Day

Materials: "Sequencing My Day" pattern page (page 94), scissors, glue, crayons, 3 x 18 strip of construction paper

1. Make a copy of the "Sequencing My Day" pattern page for each child.
2. Have the children color the page. Separate the squares on the dotted lines. Ask the children to paste the pictures in order from the start of the day to the end of the day on the paper strips.
3. Tell the children to circle or place an X by the time of day they like best.

Check for Understanding

- Time is measured in seconds, minutes, and hours.
- Our days are filled with routines.

Clockwork Pattern Page

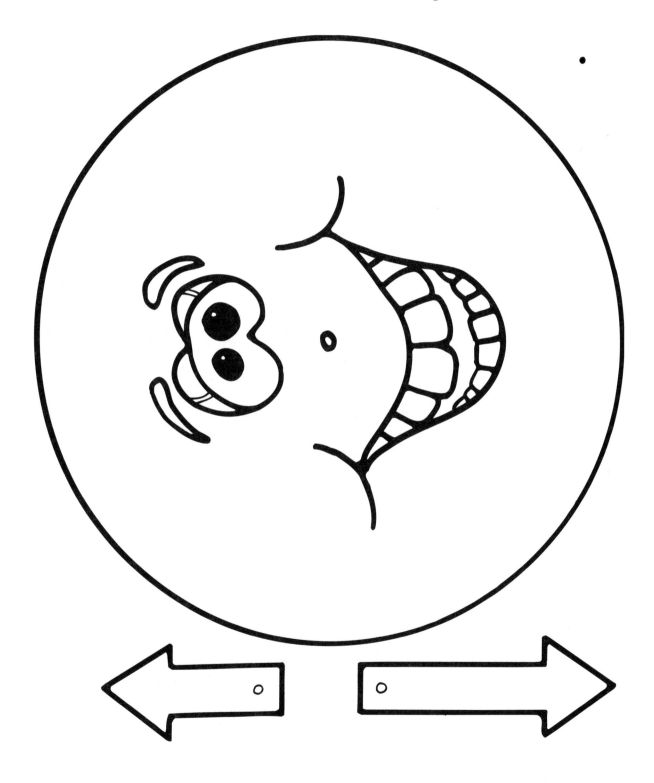

0-7682-2810-7 *Learning Basic Vocabulary*

Name_____

Sequencing My Day Pattern Page

0-7682-2810-7 *Learning Basic Vocabulary*

Days of the Week

Words to know: week, Sunday, Monday, Tuesday, Wednesday, Thursday, Friday, Saturday

Overview: Just as our time is sequenced from morning until night, our days are sequenced into a week.

Seven Days

Materials: days of the week flash cards, resealable plastic bags, paper, pencils

1. Make a copy of the days of the week flash cards for each child. Separate and place the cards in a resealable bag for safekeeping.

2. Help the children learn the names and the order of the week by singing this simple "Days of the Week" song.

"Days of the Week" (sung to "Mary Had a Little Lamb")

Seven days are in a week, in a week, in a week.

Seven days are in a week. This is what I know.

Sunday, Monday, then Tuesday

And Wednesday and Thursday,

Friday followed by Saturday,

Those are the days of the week.

3. Repeat the song, each time humming the name of one of the days instead of singing it. See if the class can discover which day you left out.

4. Have the children fold a sheet of paper in half, in half again, then in half one more time to create eight spaces separated by creases. Open the paper, and write their name and the numbers 1–7 in a column down the left-hand side of the paper, one number in between each crease.

5. Have the children remove the days of the week flash cards from their bags. Hold up the flash card that says "Sunday." Have the children find the matching flash card from their pile. Place the "Sunday" flash card next to the number 1 on the folded sheet of paper. Continue until all of the flash cards are on the sheet of paper. Sing the song again, pointing to each word as it is sung.

95 0-7682-2810-7 *Learning Basic Vocabulary*

summer   flag   apple   me   snowflake   penny   clock

What Is Monday?

Materials: large copy of one week of a calendar, markers

1. Did you know that there haven't always been seven days in a week? Some cultures have had as few as four days, and other cultures have had many more. Did you know that the days of the week got their names from the Greek gods? See *Blue Monday and Friday the Thirteenth,* by Lila Perl (Clarion Books, 1986), for more interesting facts, poems, and folklore about the days of the week.

2. People often have interesting thoughts and ideas about the days of the week. For instance, Sunday is a day when many children go to church. For school children, Saturday is usually a day off. Saturday is known as a day to go shopping, run errands, or clean the house. Talk about other days.

3. Place a large copy of a one-week calendar on a poster board. Make sure the days of the week are labeled at the top of the calendar.

4. Have the children reflect on all of the things they do on Monday. How does Monday feel? Write *Monday* in the calendar space for Monday. Then write three descriptive words to describe Monday. For instance, Monday might be a sleepy day because it's hard to start back to school after the weekend. Perhaps it has rained often on Mondays in your area, so the children might remember Monday as rainy. Monday might also be the day to return books to the library. Write *sleepy, rainy, library day* under *Monday.* Rewrite *Monday* below the descriptive words. Repeat for the rest of the days of the week to create days of the week poems. Reread all of the poems to the class.

5. Read *Today Is Monday,* by Eric Carle (Philomel Books, 1988). Rewrite the text so that each day is associated with a different food to create a fun days-of-the-week snack to be served and shared while reading your adaptation.

Monday is...

... school day
... library day
... slow day

Check for Understanding

- There are seven days in a week.
- The children can properly sequence the days of the week.

0-7682-2810-7 *Learning Basic Vocabulary*

Name_____

My Week Is ... Pattern Page

 **Monday**

 **Tuesday**

 Wednesday

Name_____

My Week Is ... Pattern Page

 **Thursday**

 **Friday**

 **Saturday**

 **Sunday**

clock   penny   snowflake   me   apple

flag

Months of the Year

Words to know: year, month, January, February, March, April, May, June, July, August, September, October, November, December

Overview: There are 12 months in a year. Each month has special days and holidays.

A Month of Sundays

Materials: months of the year flash cards, 12 cardboard boxes, assortment of objects that are symbolic of the different months (suggested items: hearts; snowman; umbrella; pictures of Martin Luther King, Jr., George Washington, Abraham Lincoln; valentines; shamrocks; etc.)

1. Months were created as the period of time it took for the moon to pass through all of its phases. You may have noticed that some nights the moon is big and round. We call this the full moon. On other nights, the moon looks as though it is being eaten away because you can see only a small sliver of it. We call these moons half, quarter, and crescent moons. Read *Papa, Please Get the Moon For Me,* by Eric Carle (Little Simon, 1999), for a good illustration of the phases of the moon. The period of time between full moons is about 30 days, so this, very simplistically speaking, is how the year got divided into months. For more information about the months of the year, the meaning of their names, and other interesting facts, see *The Months of the Year,* by Paul Hughes (Garrett Educational Corp., 1989).

2. Each of the months has a different name. Each month is unique due to seasonal and weather patterns and special days and holidays that are celebrated.

3. Read *Chicken Soup with Rice,* by Maurice Sendak (Harper Trophy, 1991), or *A Busy Year,* by Leo Lionni (Alfred A. Knopf, Inc., 1992). After reading about each month, stop and place on the board the flash card with the month's name. List the characteristics the children recall from the book.

summer   triangle   mother   eyes   planet   leaf

0-7682-2810-7 *Learning Basic Vocabulary*

summer flag apple me snowflake penny clock

4. Label each box with a different flash card. Have the children sort through the collection of items you gathered that are symbolic of the weather or special days of each month. Have the children choose an item, tell what it represents to them, and explain why they are placing it in a particular box.

Extension: Have each child stand up when you call out the name of the month he or she was born. Give the children a round of applause and shout "Happy Birthday."

Extension: Have each child draw one of the months of the year flash cards from your hands. Help him or her make up a dance or movement activity that reflects or expresses the month. See if the other children can guess by the charade which month the child is trying to portray.

Months of the Year Card Games

Materials: "Months of the Year" pattern pages (pages 101–102), markers, scissors

1. On card stock, make two copies of each of the "Months of the Year" pattern pages. Color as desired, cut out, and laminate.

2. Use the cards for the following games:

Matching: Lay all of the cards facedown on the table. Have the children take turns selecting cards and making matches. At the end of the game, ask the children to put all of the cards in order.

Silly Slap: Make two to four additional copies of the cards. Shuffle the cards and deal them so all players have an equal number of cards. Hold the stack of cards facedown so you cannot see the words or pictures. The object is to collect all of the cards in the deck. Alternating turns, pull the card from the top of your deck and place it faceup on the table. Continue alternating turns until someone places a card from the current month on top of the pile of cards. The first person to slap the top of the discard pile gets all of the cards and adds them to the bottom of his or her pile. Continue playing until one person collects all of the cards.

Name _____

Months of the Year Pattern Page

January

February

March

April

May

June

0-7682-2810-7 *Learning Basic Vocabulary*

Name _____

Months of the Year Pattern Page

July

August

September

October

November

December

0-7682-2810-7 *Learning Basic Vocabulary*

clock penny  snowflake me apple

Seasons

Words to know: seasons, spring, summer, autumn, winter

Overview: There are four seasons in the year: winter, spring, summer, and autumn. Each season is marked by different changes. The clothing people wear, the activities humans and animals engage in, the foods people eat, and the plants that grow all indicate the season of the year.

Mixed-up Seasons

Materials: assortment of clothing and accessories that are indicative of different seasons, four large boxes—each labeled with a different season, season words flash cards

1. Select four children to be your "models." Dress each child with a mixture of assorted seasonal clothing and accessories. Continue until you have dressed all four children with mixed-up seasonal gear.

2. Have the children parade in front of the class and ask the class if they notice anything peculiar about their classmates.

3. Talk about how our clothing, our activities, and the world around us change with the seasons. Choose four other children and place a season word flash card on each child to label him or her as "spring," "summer," "autumn," or "winter."

4. Choose one child to remove an article from one of the mixed-up season children and place the item on the child with correct season label. Repeat until all of the children are sorted correctly.

5. Talk about the different seasons and the clothing, accessories, and props that are associated with each season.

Extension: Divide the class into four teams. Make certain you have an equal number of clothing, props, and accessories for each season and at least one item per team member. Place the boxes at one end of the room and the teams at the other end. At your signal, each team sends one person at a time to select one item from the box and put it on. The child then returns to the group and tags the next player, who then races to the box for the next item. The children continue racing until one team has emptied its box.

summer

flag

apple

me

snowflake

penny

clock

Season Sorting

Materials: clothing, accessories, props from the previous activity, paper, crayons

Have the children take turns sorting all of the seasonal wear into the appropriate box. Choose a second child to check the accuracy of the first child's sorting. Then have the children draw a picture of their favorite season. (They may want to include some of the items from the boxes.) Have them write or dictate a story about their pictures.

Check for Understanding

- We have four seasons.
- Our clothing, the weather, and our activities reflect changes in the seasons.

What Makes Spring, Spring?

Materials: "Spring Things" pattern page (page 107), scissors, basket, 6 small box lids for sorting patterns

What makes spring, spring? Spring is the season when:

- Birds migrate.
- Baby animals are born.
- Grass, leaves, and other plants and flowers begin to grow.
- The air begins to get warmer.
- Days are getting longer.
- It is often rainy.
- You can trade your winter coat for a light jacket or sweater.
- It is time to clean up yards and homes after a long winter's sleep.

1. Read *Hopper Hunts for Spring,* by Marcus Pfister (North-South Books 1995), *When Spring Comes,* by Robert Maass (Henry Holt, 1994), or another book that illustrates spring. If it is currently the spring season, check the environment around you for signs of spring. Copy the list above on poster board, decorate with spring symbols, and display in a prominent place.

2. Make several copies of the "Spring Things" pattern page on colored paper. Cut out the objects and place them in a basket.

3. Have the children sit in a circle. Select one child to be the "Spring Flinger" who skips around the circle of children showering them with the pattern pieces.

4. Have the children gather the items and place them on the ground. Count the total number.

5. At the top of a blackboard or dry-erase board, write, "In our spring garden, we found …"

6. Have the children help you find a descriptive word for worms, such as "wiggly." Below the first line, write "_____ wiggly worms."

7. Select two children to bring all of the worms they collected to the middle of the circle. Have the first child count his or her worms. Write that number on the board. Have the second child count his or her worms. Write that number on the board. Now add the two sets of worms together by "counting on" to get a total number of worms. Finish the math sentence on the board by writing a + and = symbol to the numbers you have written. Add the total number of worms counted to the sentence describing the worms.

flag summer triangle mother eyes planet leaf

8. Repeat with two more children and a second set of spring things.

9. Once you have completed this with all of the spring things, read your "In our spring garden" message. Then begin again until everyone has had a chance to count, add, and contribute.

In our spring garden, we found...

  5   Wiggly worms 🪱

  7   pretty flowers 🌸

  4   drippy drops 💧

  6   fancy umbrellas ☂

Spring Patterning

Materials: Spring Thing symbols collected in boxes in previous activity, 12 x 18 pieces of construction paper folded in half the long way, glue, crayons

1. On the top half of each piece of paper write patterning directions such as ABAB, ABB, and AAB.

2. Have the children choose a piece of paper and glue the spring symbols above the fold, according to the pattern suggested at the top.

3. Next, have the child choose a different patterning sequence and glue on the spring symbols in that pattern below the fold.

Wildflower Prints

Materials: assortment of wildflowers, hammers or rubber mallets, paper

1. Place a wildflower between two sheets of paper.

2. Lightly pound the paper with a hammer around the area where the wildflower is positioned.

3. Lift the top sheet and peel away what is left of the wildflower. Repeat as desired to make your own wildflower printed paper. Use the paper for framing a picture, cut and fold to use as note cards, or use for book covers.

Check for Understanding

- Spring is a time for new growth and warmer weather.
- Many things around us are symbols (or remind us) of spring.

Name _____

Spring Things Pattern Page

0-7682-2810-7 *Learning Basic Vocabulary*

summer

flag

apple

me

snowflake

penny

clock

What Makes Summer, Summer?

Materials: large map, postcards, stickers

Discuss: What makes summer, summer? Summer is the season for:

- Hot weather.
- Sunny days.
- Swimming, fishing, and other activities for lazy summer days.
- Summer vacation.
- Swimsuits and sandals.
- Cold treats.

1. A few days before this lesson, send home a note requesting postcards from previous vacations (or clip pictures from travel brochures and magazines). Encourage each child to bring a summer item or memento from home to share.

2. Read *When Summer Comes,* by Robert Maass (Henry Holt & Co., 1996). Talk about the sights, smells, and sounds of summertime. If it is currently the summer season, check the environment around you for signs of summer. Copy the list above (adding other ideas if you wish) onto poster board, decorate with summer symbols, and display.

3. Talk about how summer is traditionally the time of year when we take a break from school and work to recreate.

4. Show each postcard, asking the children if they think it looks like someplace they would like to travel in the summertime. Talk about the different kinds of things they would need to pack for a trip to the beach, to the mountains for camping, or to an amusement park.

5. Encourage the children to share their favorite vacation.

Extension: On a large map, mark the cities where the children have vacationed in past summers. Note how many vacationed close to home and how many vacationed farther away.

clock  penny snowflake me apple

flag

summer

triangle

mother

eyes

planet

leaf

My Favorite Summer Activity

Materials: 9 x 12 pieces of construction paper, "My Summer Activity" pattern page (page 110), markers, glue

1. Make a copy of the "My Summer Activity" pattern page for each child. Have the children draw a picture of their summer vacation or of a summer vacation they would like to take.

2. Have each child write or dictate a story about his or her favorite thing to do in the summertime.

3. Mount the picture on a sheet of construction paper to frame the work.

4. Create a "Summertime Museum" from the postcards, mementos, and pictures that the children created.

Summer Sun Fade Art

Materials: assortment of die cuts of familiar objects, letters, numbers, envelopes, tape, colored construction paper that is *not* labeled as "fadeless"

1. Let each child choose three or four items from the assortment of die cuts.

2. Tape the die cuts to a sheet of construction paper (dark colors produce more vivid effects). Make sure that none of the die cuts overlap.

3. Tape the pictures to a sunny window, die cut side facing out. Leave the pictures in the window for a couple of weeks.

4. After removing the pictures from the windows, remove the taped die cuts and place them in an envelope taped to the back of the picture.

5. Read *Shapes and Things,* by Tana Hoban (Simon and Schuster, 1991). Discuss how the children can identify objects by their shapes. As you present the pictures to the class, explain how they can use the heat and light from the sun to create shapes. Show the faded pictures to the class and see if they can identify which die cuts were used.

Check for Understanding

- Summer is a time for hot weather and activities that keep us cool.

Name _____

My Summer Activity Pattern Page

0-7682-2810-7 *Learning Basic Vocabulary*

What Makes Autumn, Autumn?

Materials: Leaf pattern page (page 113), spray adhesive, scissors, large sheet of brown craft paper

1. Make a copy of the Leaf pattern page on four pieces of green paper. Using spray adhesive, take a yellow, orange, brown, and red piece of paper and glue each one to the back of a green pattern page. Cut the leaves out to create individual leaves with green on one side and yellow, red, orange, or brown on the reverse side. Laminate for durability.

2. Draw a small tree trunk on a large sheet of brown butcher paper. Tape each leaf onto the tree, green side showing.

Discuss: What makes autumn, autumn? Autumn is the season for:

- Leaves changing color.
- Cooler temperatures.
- First frosts.
- Sweaters and football games.
- Harvesting crops.
- Migrating birds.
- Cleaning up and storing things for the winter.

3. Read *When Autumn Comes,* by Robert Maass (Henry Holt & Co., 1992), or other books that depict the changes in autumn. Talk about the signs of autumn. If it is currently the autumn season, check the environment around you for signs of autumn. Copy the list above (adding other ideas if you wish) onto poster board, decorate with autumn symbols, and display.

4. Read *Why Do Leaves Change Colors,* by Betsy Maestro (Harper Trophy, 1994). Reinforce words such as *chlorophyll* and the concept that the leaves are not really changing colors, but are simply loosing the green color due to a lack of chlorophyll.

summer
flag
apple
me
snowflake
penny
clock

Let each child have the opportunity to remove a leaf from the tree. Then have the whole class chant and move according to the color revealed on the back of the leaf. Each leaf has its own action associated with a color:

- Yellow: Everyone stands up; turns in a circle chanting "mellow, mellow yellow;" and then sits back down.

- Red: Everyone stomps his or her feet on the ground at the same time while chanting "r-r-red," "r-r-red."

- Orange: Everyone claps once then whispers "orange," claps again and whispers "owls," claps again and whispers "overhead."

- Brown: Everyone stands up and pats his or her legs while chanting "Brown, brown, brown starts with B-B-B."

Changing Leaves

Materials: red, yellow, orange, and brown crayons; Leaf Pattern page (page 113); green tempera paint; paint smocks; brushes; coins

1. Make a copy of the Leaf pattern page (page 113) for each child. Have students color each of the leaves using autumn-colored crayons. Encourage the children to color with heavy lines so the whole leaf is covered with thick wax.

2. Paint over the entire page with green tempera paint and allow to dry.

3. When completely dry, use the edge of a coin to scrape the paint off the picture where the leaves are.

Autumn Patterning

Materials: assortment of natural autumn objects such as small colored leaves and acorns, 3 x 5 cards with patterning sequences (AABB, ABC, AAB, etc.) written on them, card stock cut in thirds the long way, glue

1. Have each child choose a patterning sequence card.

2. Using the 3 x 5 pattern sequencing cards, create patterns with the autumn nature objects by gluing the objects in order on card stock.

Check for Understanding

- There are many signs of autumn.

- Leaves change color because they stop producing chlorophyll due to a lack of sunlight.

Name_____

Leaf Pattern Page

triangle △   mother   eyes 👁👁   planet 🪐   leaf 🍂

summer

flag
apple
me
snowflake

penny

clock

What Makes Winter, Winter?

Materials: "Snowflake" pattern page (page 116), scissors, marker, tissue paper

1. Use the "Snowflake" pattern page as a template for making snowflakes out of tissue paper. Cut tissue paper to size using the dotted square. Fold the square sheet of tissue in half across the diagonal as shown. Then fold this triangle into thirds (see illustration on pattern page). Place one of the snowflake patterns on top of the folded tissue paper and cut on the dotted lines (or cut your own pattern). Make one snowflake for each child.

2. Write simple math sentences such as "1 + 2 =" on one snowflake and "3" on another. Or for a simpler activity, draw dots on one snowflake and a corresponding number on another. Continue creating number pairs until you have enough for the entire class.

3. Discuss what makes winter, winter? Winter is the season for:

- Cold air.
- Snow, sleet, and icicles.
- Snowmen.
- Sledding, hockey, and ice skating.
- Mittens and hats.
- Hibernating.
- Warm fires and hot chocolate.

4. Read *When Winter Comes,* by Robert Maass (Henry Holt & Co., 1993). Talk about the signs of winter. If it is currently the winter season, check the environment around you for signs of winter. Copy the list above (adding other ideas if you wish) onto poster board, decorate with winter symbols, and display in a prominent place.

5. Give each child a prepared snowflake. Show an example of the snowflake matches.

6. Tell the children that you are about to have a winter storm in class and all of the snowflakes will be blown about and mixed up as a result. You'll need their help to set things straight.

7. At your signal, have the children carry away all of the snowflakes, as if blown about in a storm. As you signal the class again, have them float their snowflakes around the room in search of their snowflake match. Tell the children that once they find one another, the partners should float to the ground and sit down until all of the children have found their snowflake matches.

clock   penny   snowflake  me   apple

Snowflake Storm

Materials: tissue paper, pencils, scissors, black construction paper, white tempera paint, glue

1. Fold the tissue paper as directed previously to begin a snowflake. Have the children trace shapes on the tissue paper for cutting or have them use the snowflake templates provided by taping them on top of the folded tissue paper.

2. After unfolding the snowflake, carefully glue it to a piece of black construction paper. After dipping the pencil eraser into white tempera paint, dot as many "snowflakes" as desired around the snowflake on the dark paper. After the paint has dried, see if you can count all of the snowflakes in your snowstorm.

Snowflake Crystals

Materials: large clear plastic drinking glasses, epsom salts, hot water, pipe cleaners, string, craft sticks, plastic spoons, towels (for clean up)

1. Cut the pipe cleaners into thirds. Give each child three pieces. Show the children how to twist the pieces together through the middle to create a six-stemmed snowflake frame as shown. Tie a piece of string around one of the ends and around a craft stick. Label the craft stick with the child's name. Label the plastic cup with the child's name.

2. Fill the cup 2/3 full of hot water. Have the children spoon epsom salts into the hot water and stir until dissolved. Have them continue adding salt until no more can be dissolved in the water and it continues to fall out to the bottom of the cup.

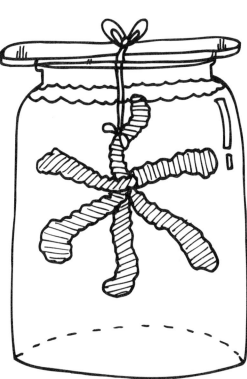

3. Ask the children to predict what will happen to the snowflake frame when it is placed in the solution. Carefully immerse the snowflake frame into the solution and place the craft stick across the top of the cup.

4. Place the cup in a safe place for a day or two and watch what happens!

5. Hang your crystal snowflakes from the ceiling.

0-7682-2810-7 *Learning Basic Vocabulary*

Name _____

Snowflake Pattern Page

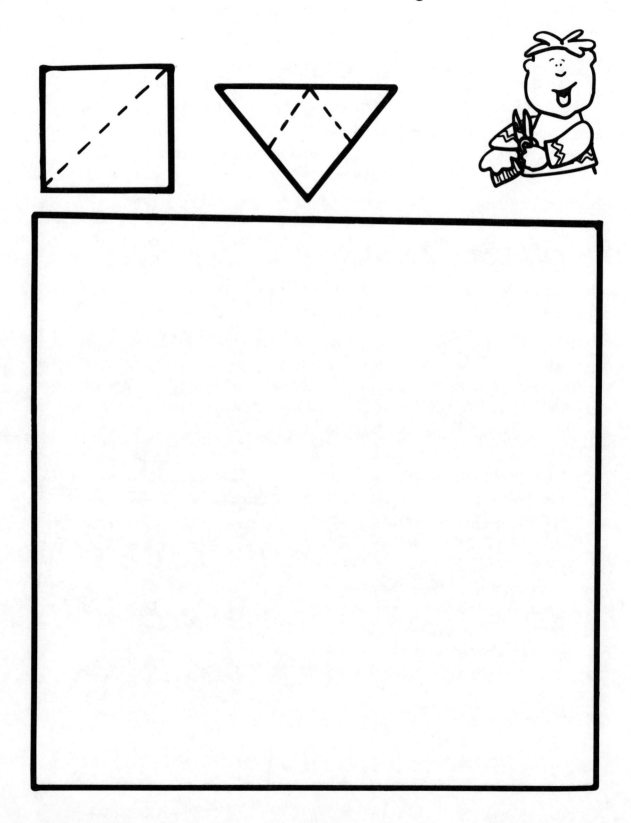

0-7682-2810-7 *Learning Basic Vocabulary*

Weather

Words to know: weather, sunny, rainy, cloudy, windy, foggy, snowy, hot, cold, temperature

Overview: Weather changes occur from day to day and across the seasons. These changes affect what people wear and what activities they pursue. It is important to be aware of the weather in order to be prepared and to stay safe.

Weather Watchers

Materials: video of a TV weather forecast, TV/VCR, several copies of the weather word flash cards (cut out and laminated), monthly calendar, graphing chart, outdoor mercury and digital thermometers

1. Videotape a local weather forecast the night before this lesson. Begin the lesson by showing the tape. What was the forecast for today? Based on current weather conditions, was the weather report accurate?

2. Have the children consider the importance of accurate weather predictions. Tell the children that knowing the weather forecast helps them appropriately plan the activities of the day, and what they will wear.

3. Weather patterns are fairly consistent throughout each season. It is not unusual to have snow or rain and cold temperatures in the winter. It is unusual to experience these kinds of weather events in summer. Have the children predict the next day's weather based on the current weather patterns and season.

4. Have one child be your weather watcher. Send him or her outside with a partner to assess the weather and check the temperature. Keep a record of the weather for a month by taping to a calendar the appropriate weather word flash card that describes the day's dominant weather. At the end of the month, graph the weather patterns by transferring the weather flash cards to a bar graph. As the year passes, can the children see a change in the weather? As you celebrate your hundredth day of school, make a graph of all of the weather days up to that point.

triangle △   mother    eyes 👁👁   planet 🪐   leaf 🍂

 summer

Extension: Keep track of the weather forecast and the actual weather for a couple of weeks. How accurate is the weather forecasting in your area?

Musical Storms

Materials: assortment of percussion instruments: sticks, blocks, drums, cymbals, and triangles

1. Give each child a musical instrument.

2. Talk about rainstorms. Note how they usually start out slow with just a few drops of rain falling at a time. Invite the children with wooden sticks to softly, slowly tap their sticks together.

3. After a few minutes, the rain clouds move closer and more rain begins to fall. Invite those who are playing blocks to join in by quickly rubbing the blocks together. (The sticks continue to tap more rapidly.)

4. Finally, the rain moves in, and there are thunder claps (drums) and lightning crashes (cymbals). Encourage all of the children to play vigorously.

5. At your signal, the drums and lightning cease (drums and cymbals stop playing), the rain continues to lighten (blocks stop rubbing), and the rain slows to a stop.

6. Now all you can hear are footsteps splashing in puddles (triangles).

7. Exchange instruments and begin a new thunderstorm.

Extension: The next time a rainstorm happens on a school day, open the windows, turn out the lights, lie on the floor, and LISTEN to the rain.

Extension: Consider these suggestions to further explore the weather:

• Use a box fan to explore the effects of wind and things that blow.

• Wait for a snowy day and use a yardstick to measure the snow drifts in different locations around the school. Record the results and compare them with a recent snowstorm.

• Read *It Looked Like Spilt Milk*, by Charles G. Shaw (Harper Collins, 1993). Lie on the grass to observe the clouds. Create your own cloud pictures with stretched cotton.

Stormy Weather Game

Materials: weather word flash cards, "Stormy Weather" pattern pages (pages 120-121), file folder, markers, die, resealable plastic bag, 4 small tokens

1. Make five copies of the weather word flash cards on card stock. Cut out and laminate.

2. Make a copy of the "Stormy Weather" pattern pages. Color as desired. Paste to the inside of a file folder to create a game board.

3. Reproduce the directions below and paste them on the outside of the folder. Laminate for durability.

4. Staple the bag to the outside of the game board to hold the game pieces.

To play: The object of the game is to be the first to move your token around the board from school to home, avoiding as much bad weather as possible.

1. Shuffle the weather word flash cards and place them facedown where indicated on the game board.

2. Take turns rolling the die and moving your token the number of spaces indicated.

3. If you land on a weather space, tell one thing you know about that kind of weather.

4. If you land on a counting space, follow the directions on the space.

5. If you land on a "take a card" space, you must draw a card from the weather card pile. If you draw a cloudy card, simply return it to the bottom of the stack.

6. If you draw a sunny card, move ahead one space. Return the card to the bottom of the stack.

7. If you draw a foggy card, everyone gets up and changes places around the board as if you are lost in a fog. (Continue playing in the new order.)

8. If you draw a rainy card, move back one space; a windy card, back two spaces; and a snowy card, back three spaces.

Check for Understanding

- Knowing what the weather is can help us plan what to wear and what activities we can do.

flag summer triangle mother eyes planet leaf

Name_____

Stormy Weather Pattern Page

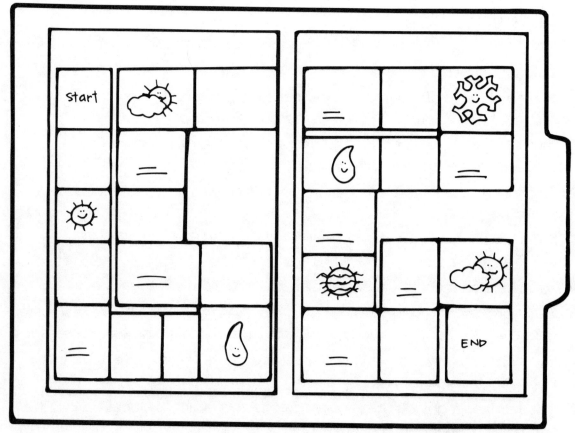

Name_____

Stormy Weather Pattern Page

"Start"

box #1

Foggy

box #20

Stormy Weather Game

Count to 10

box #2

High "5"

box #19

Snowy Day

box #3, 23

Say Name

box #13

Rainy Day

box #9, 14

Sunny Day

box #11, 18

Pick a Card

box #
5, 10, 15, 17, 22, 25

Cloudy Day

box #6, 16

Hop on 1 Foot

box #7

0-7682-2810-7 *Learning Basic Vocabulary*

triangle △   mother 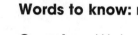   eyes 👁👁   planet 🪐   leaf 🍃

 summer

My World

Words to know: recycling, resources

Overview: Water, rocks, soil, and living things are found on the earth's surface. We use the earth's resources every day. Some resources can be renewed, while others get used up. Many resources can be conserved.

Our Earth's Natural Resources

Take a walk exploring nature around you. Discuss the differences between living and nonliving things. Does something that is living feel different from something that is nonliving? Feel the grass and a concrete sidewalk. Compare the feel of carpet to your skin. See if you can locate some of the earth's natural resources, such as a stream, a pond, or another form of water; a tree or other living and growing things; and air.

Can you find examples of people using resources in and around your school? Is the cook using water to make lunch? Are the children in class using paper and books? Are the lights on?

What's a Kindergartner To Do?

Air, water, plants, and soil are all natural resources. They are important to our health and well-being. Being a responsible member of a community means doing our best to conserve these resources.

Energy Resources. Most of the energy you use today comes from fossil fuels. Producing oil and gas from fossil fuels not only uses up a natural resource that cannot be reproduced, but also creates pollution. Scientists are working to find other ways of providing energy that costs less to produce and that doesn't pollute. Using the wind, using steam from geothermal springs, turning rotting garbage into gas, and creating new forms of fuel will help conserve our natural resources. What's a kindergartner to do? Encourage the children to think of ways they can conserve energy. Some ideas to get you started: walk, ride your bike, and turn out the lights.

flag  apple  me snowflake penny  clock

clock · penny · snowflake · me · apple

Biofuel

Materials: food scraps, resealable plastic bags

1. Create your own biofuel by gathering food scraps in resealable plastic bags.

2. Make a prediction of what you think will happen in and to the bags.

3. Place the bags in a warm sunny place for a couple of days. Watch what happens. (The bag will begin to puff up.) That's not air in there! That's methane gas produced by the many organisms that are eating up what's left of the scraps.

4. Throw the bags away. Do not open the bags.

Recycling. Many people are interested in recycling. However, we are throwing out a lot more trash than we used to. What's a kindergartner to do? Be your family's recycling officer and watch for things going out in the trash that can be recycled. Save containers and products that can be used over again.

As a class, start an aluminum can recycling campaign. Advertise to the other classes and send notes home to the parents. Use the proceeds from recycling the aluminum cans to buy a new tree for the school.

Preserving our forests. Trees are very important to the environment. They help clean the air, give birds and animals homes to live, and help keep the soil from eroding. Trees are cut down for making lumber for homes and buildings and for making paper. Trees are a natural resource that can be reproduced, but it takes many years for a tree to grow to replace one that has been chopped down. What's a kindergartner to do? Save paper. Use both sides of a piece of paper. Recycle the paper when you do use it.

flag · summer · triangle · mother · eyes · planet · leaf

0-7682-2810-7 *Learning Basic Vocabulary*

Recycled Paper

Materials: bucket, water, stiff wire screen, construction paper scraps, large stirring stick, paper towels

1. Using construction paper scraps, tear them into little pieces and place them in a big bucket of warm water.

2. Soak the paper scraps overnight.

3. Blend the pulp by stirring it with a big stick (or divide it among the children and have each of them stir his or her own bowl of pulp).

4. Add about a gallon of water, stirring it into the paper pulp to make a thin slurry.

5. Over a sink or outdoors, pour the slurry in a thin layer over a stiff wire screen. Let it dry for about an hour.

6. Quickly and carefully tip the screen over onto paper towels. Blot off the back of the screen and peel it away from the sheet of paper.

7. Let your recycled paper air-dry overnight and use it for a special project.

Earth Recycling Collage

Materials: "Earth Recycling Collage" pattern page (page 125); glue; assortment of recyclable materials such as magazines, newspaper, milk cartons, and foam containers; scissors

1. Make a copy of the "Earth Recycling Collage" pattern page for each child.

2. Have the children cut small sections from a variety of recyclable materials.

3. Using the picture of the earth on the pattern page, glue the materials on the earth. Try to cover the water with one type of material, the border with another and the landforms with still another.

Check for Understanding

• The earth has many natural resources.

• We can conserve these resources by being conscious of our consumption and conservation.

Name_____

Earth Recycling Collage Pattern Page

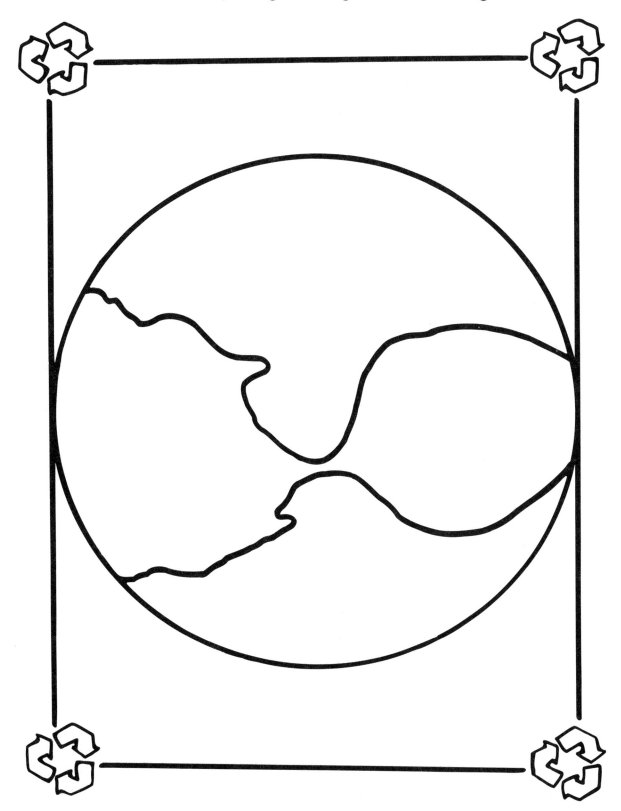

0-7682-2810-7 *Learning Basic Vocabulary*

triangle △   mother   eyes 👁👁   planet 🪐   leaf 🍂

 summer

 flag

 apple

 me

 snowflake

 penny

 clock

Space

Words to know: star, planet, sun, moon, Mercury, Venus, Earth, Mars, Jupiter, Saturn, Uranus, Pluto

Overview: All of the planets in our solar system orbit around the sun. Some planets have no moons. Others have many. Earth has one moon. The sun is a star. All of the other stars are far away, but they can be seen at night when the sun is no longer in the sky.

Planets

Materials: copies of the "Solar System" pattern pages (pages 130–132), flashlight, basketball, ping-pong ball, watermelon, small lime, 2 grapes, honeydew melon, 2 medium-sized apples, 2 oranges

1. Make a copy of the "Solar System" pattern pages. Color, cut out, and laminate for durability.

2. Turn on the flashlight. Explain that this flashlight represents the sun. It shines on the earth. Hold the basketball up so it is in the path of the light from the flashlight. Note that only one side of the ball is illuminated. Discuss how the side of the ball (or earth) that is light is similar to the earth during the daytime. Make an X on the ball and slowly rotate it around so the X moves from the light to the shaded side of the ball. This side represents the earth at night.

3. Have a child hold the basketball while you add a ping-pong ball to represent the moon. The moon orbits around the earth. Sometimes the moon is in between the earth and the sun. Other times it catches the full light of the sun. This is why there is a full, half, and crescent moon.

4. Line up the fruit in the following order: grape, orange, orange, lime, watermelon, honeydew melon, apple, apple, grape.

5. Explain that these fruits are approximate representations of the size differences between the planets. Place the picture of Mercury below the grape, Venus and Earth below the oranges, Mars below the lime, Jupiter below the watermelon, Saturn below the honeydew melon, Uranus and Neptune below the apples, and Pluto below the grape. Compare the size differences between the biggest and the smallest planets.

clock    penny   snowflake ✳   me   apple

6. Share a few interesting facts about each planet:

- **Mercury** is the planet that is closest to the sun. Mercury has no atmosphere so it has no way to keep heat. Even though it is closest to the sun, the side that faces away from the sun freezes completely, only to be reheated to super hot temperatures during the day.

- **Venus** rotates counterclockwise so the sun rises in the west and sets in the east. Most of the planet is covered with volcanic rock. Because of its atmosphere, Venus is the hottest planet in the solar system.

- **Earth** is the planet we call home. The temperature is just right for sustaining life. If the earth were any closer or any further from the sun, life would not be possible.

- **Mars** is called the Red Planet because the type of rocks that are found there look red. Mars has very thin air, so the further away from the surface, the colder it gets.

- **Jupiter** is the largest planet. In fact, all of the other planets could fit inside Jupiter with room to spare. Jupiter has many windstorms, some lasting for many years.

- **Saturn** is famous for its rings. The rings are actually a bunch of rocks and ice that rotate around the planet. Saturn is a gas planet, which means that it is made up of gas, not dirt and rocks.

- **Uranus** also has rings, although they are not as spectacular as Saturn's. Uranus is tipped on its side, which means that summer and winter seem to last forever.

- **Neptune** looks blue. Neptune is also a very windy planet. The wind races around the planet in the opposite direction that it spins. If you were to live on Neptune, there would be no sense in combing your hair and every day would be a kite-flying day.

- **Pluto** is the smallest planet. It is also the planet that is farthest away from the sun. Pluto's orbit around the sun takes it inside the orbit of Neptune for a while. For 20 years of every 248, Pluto is not the farthest from the sun.

summer

flag

apple

me

snowflake

penny

clock

How Far to the Sun?

Materials: "Solar System" pattern pages (pages 130–132), 3.5' diameter circle cut from yellow craft paper (laminated), tape measure

1. Choose one child to be each of the planets. Give each child one of the prepared planet pictures from the planet pattern pages. You will need two children to hold the 3.5' diameter craft paper circle that represents the sun. Use the extra children in the class to be stars, moons, and the asteroid belt.

2. Go outside where you have a long field you can use. Have the children who are holding the sun stand at one end of the field. Place the rest of the planets as listed below:

   - Mercury   9" from the sun
   - Venus   1' from the sun
   - Earth   1 1/2' from the sun
   - Mars   2 1/2' from the sun

Asteroid belt: Place several children between Mars and Jupiter to demonstrate the asteroid belt—a band of asteroids that separates the first four planets from the others.

   - Jupiter   8' from the sun
   - Saturn   15' from the sun
   - Uranus   30' from the sun
   - Neptune   45' from the sun
   - Pluto   73' from the sun
   - Stars   Have any remaining children stand in random spots around the field past Pluto.

Now you can see why Pluto is so cold! You also can see why the stars seem so small. They are very far away. Make other comparisons and observations about the solar system.

clock  penny snowflake  me apple

Space Mobiles

Materials: hanger, string, "Solar System" pattern pages (pages 130–132), tape

1. Make a copy of the pattern pages for each child. Have the children color and cut out the planets.

2. Tape the sun to the middle of the hanger as shown.

3. Hang the other planets from the hanger by taping string to the back of the planet pictures and tying the other end around the hanger.

4. Arrange the planets in order. Try to extend the length of each string so that Mercury is very close to the hanger and Pluto extends farther away.

Check for Understanding

- Nine planets are in our solar system: Mercury, Venus, Earth, Mars, Jupiter, Saturn, Uranus, Neptune, and Pluto.

- The planets orbit around the earth.

- Each planet has unique characteristics, including size and distance from the sun.

flag summer triangle mother eyes planet leaf

Name_____

Solar System Pattern Page

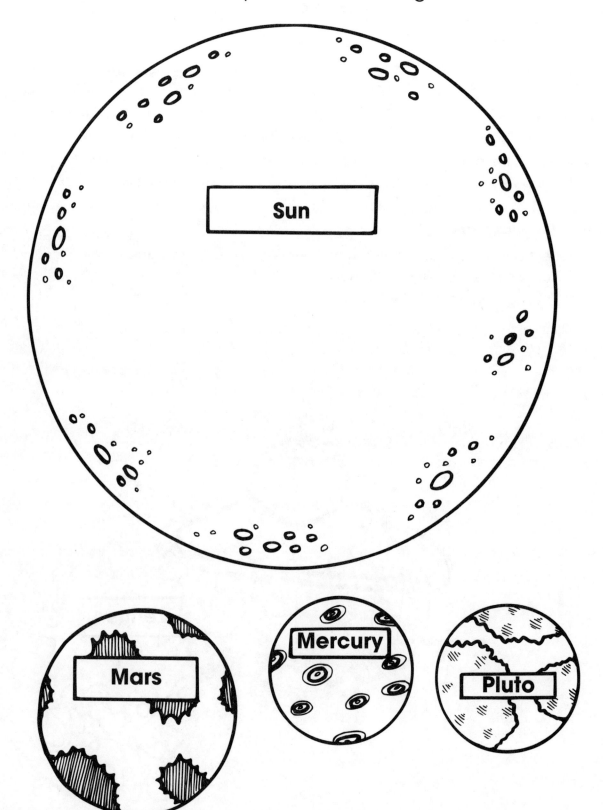

0-7682-2810-7 *Learning Basic Vocabulary*

Name _____

Solar System Pattern Page

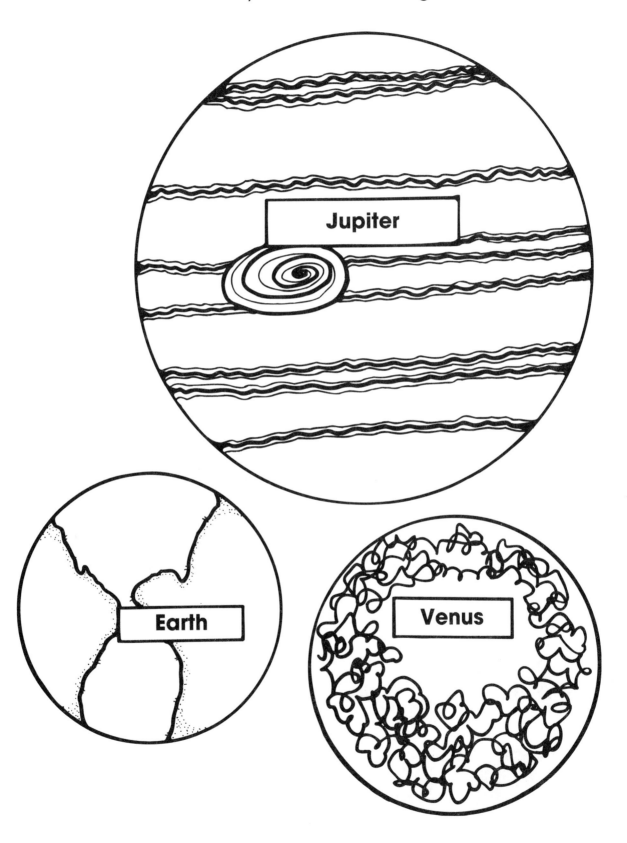

Name _____

Solar System Pattern Page

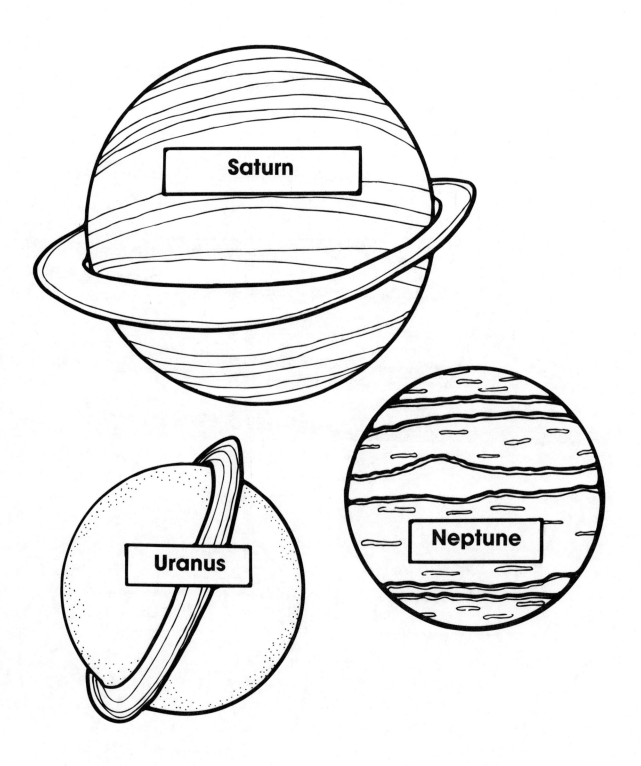

Plant Life

Words to know: leaves, roots, flowers, stem, bark

Overview: Plants are growing things that provide us with food, beauty, and shelter. The leaves, roots, flowers, stems, and bark of plants help the plant get food and water, reproduce, grow, and protect itself.

What Plants Need

Materials: cactus, water plant, flower (needing full sun), fern or other shade plant, sand, clay soil, potting soil, seeds (grass, radish, and bean)

1. Plants need good soil, water, and sunlight in order to grow.

2. We know that all plants need water. Without it, a plant eventually withers and dies. Some plants need less water than others. The Saguaro cactus can live for a very long time and thrives in conditions where there is little water. Other plants, such as seaweed, grow in the water. Seaweed needs a lot of water to live.

3. Show the cactus and the water plant. Discuss what might happen if the cactus got too much water and the water plant too little. Try your experiment over the next week and discuss and record your results.

4. All plants need sunlight. Plants make chlorophyll from sunlight, which, in turn, feeds the plant. Without sunlight, the plant will die. Sunflowers, for instance, grow best when they are in the sun all day. Other plants, such as ferns, do not like direct sunlight and will burn and die if they get too much.

5. Show the plants that require full sun or indirect light. Talk about what will happen if you switch the plants and place the fern in full sunlight and the other plant in indirect light. Watch your plants over the next week and record your results.

6. Plants need soil to grow. The soil has nutrients that feed the roots of the plants. Some soils are better than others for growing. Fill three different cups with sand, clay, and potting soil. Plant seeds in each of the three cups. Hypothesize about what you think will happen to the seeds. Watch the seeds grow over the next week and record and discuss the results. Which type of soil is best for growing a particular type of seed?

summer
flag
apple
me
snowflake
penny
clock

Little Seeds

Materials: assortment of seeds and pictures of the plants or food they come from, resealable plastic bag, small pots, potting soil

1. Read *The Tiny Seed,* by Eric Carle (Aladdin Library, 2001). Have the children recall and list the different ways the seeds did not succeed. See if they can recall the events in order.

2. Place each seed in a separate bag along with a picture or sample of the type of plant (or fruit) the seed produces.

3. Compare the different seeds. Compare the sizes of the seeds. A radish seed is very small, but an acorn is a much larger seed. Sort the seeds. Now compare the size of the plants that the seeds grow into. Do bigger seeds always grow bigger plants?

4. Slice open several different seed-bearing fruits and vegetables and compare and contrast the seeds.

5. Fill several small pots with potting soil. Plant one of each seed in a pot. Label the pots. Observe the growth of the different seeds. Ask the children to predict which one will grow the fastest, which will be the last to sprout, and which plant will grow the tallest.

Beautiful Flowers

Materials: 1 flower with a stem and leaves intact for each child, 2 or 3 potted plants, paper, crayons

1. Give each child a flower to examine for 1 minute. Ask the children to notice the size, color, and other small details they can see.

2. Have the children trace their flower on a piece of paper while you draw it on the board.

3. Start with the petals and the head of the flower. Talk about the different things the children notice about the petals. Label your flower with the word, *petal.* Have the children do the same on their paper and color the petals on the flower. Talk about how the petals are on the flower to help it attract insects for pollination.

4. Move next to the stem. Have the children find the stem on their flower. Have the children suggest ideas about the function of the stem. The stem not only gives the flower support, but it also provides a means by which the plant gets water and nutrients from the soil to the flower. Label and color the stem.

5. Color and label the leaves. Note the different sizes and shapes of the leaves. The leaves collect sunlight and turn it to chlorophyll to feed the flower.

6. Pull the plants you have gathered out of their pots. Examine the roots of each plant. Are there many roots or one big one? Color and label the roots.

Comparing Seeds

Materials: seeds, 3 x 5 cards with patterning sequences (AB, ABB, ABC, etc.) written on them

1. Use the assortment of seeds for patterning or sequencing or as tokens for simple math equations.

2. Using the resealable bags from the activity on the previous page, ask students to match the seed to its appropriate parent plant.

Check for Understanding

- We use plants for food, shelter, and clothing.

- Flowers need just the right amount of sunlight, soil, and water to grow properly.

- The petals, stem, leaves, bark, and roots are necessary to a plant's survival.

summer

flag

apple

me

snowflake

penny

clock

Animal Life

Words to know: zoo, mammal, insect, amphibian, reptile, fish, bird

Overview: Some animals are wild. They live in the oceans, jungles or savannas, forests, plains, deserts, and swamps—just about everywhere on the earth. Some animals can be tamed. We use them as pets, to assist us in work, and for transportation. We call them domestic animals. We can classify animals according to their characteristics.

What Kind of Animal Are You?

Materials: animal flash cards and "Animals" pattern pages (pages 139–144)

1. Copy and select one animal from the "Animals" pattern pages to illustrate each of the animal types listed below.

2. Animals can be classified according to their characteristics.

3. Birds *(Place a picture of a bird on the board; label it with the appropriate flash card.)* are vertebrates (a backbone), and they are covered in feathers. Birds also hatch from eggs. Have the children feel down their back. Can they feel that bumpy bone? That is their vertebrae (or their back). Suggest that maybe they are birds! Now ask if they hatched from eggs or if they are covered in feathers. If they can answer yes to these questions, they must be a bird! Ask the children if they think they are birds.

4. Insects *(Place a picture of an insect on the board; label it with the appropriate flash card.)* have three body parts—head, thorax, and abdomen—but no vertebrae. Insects also have six legs and at least one pair of wings. Have the children check for these characteristics on their body. Suggest that so far they can predict that they are not insects.

5. Fish *(Place a picture of a fish on the board; label it with the appropriate flash card.)* are vertebrates who live in the water and breathe through gills. Fish are usually covered with scales and use fins for swimming. Have the children check for gills and fins. No, they are not fish either.

6. Reptiles *(Place a picture of a reptile on the board; label it with the appropriate flash card.)* are cold-blooded animals. This means that they get the heat for their blood from outside sources. In other words, if they want to be warm, they must be in a warm environment. Reptiles also creep or crawl on the ground. Have the children assess these characteristics in themselves. Do they need to be in the sun to get their blood moving? Do they creep, crawl, or slither on the ground? No, they are probably not reptiles either.

7. Amphibians *(Place a picture of an amphibian on the board; label it with the appropriate flash card.)* are cold-blooded vertebrates with moist skin. Their babies are usually born as tadpoles that have gills and live in the water. Amphibians live on land and in the water. Have the children check for vertebrae. Have them check their skin. Is it moist? Ask them to consider whether they were born as a tadpole. They don't fit these criteria either.

8. Mammals *(Place a picture of a mammal on the board; label it with the appropriate flash card.)* have a backbone and give milk to their babies. Have the children feel down their back. Can they feel that bumpy bone? That is their vertebrae (or their back). Now ask, if their mother fed them milk when they were a baby? If they can answer yes to both of these questions, they must be a mammal.

Who's Loose in the Zoo?

Materials: "Animals" pattern pages (pages 139–144), animal word flash cards, markers, scissors, tape

1. Make a copy of the "Animals" pattern pages. Color and cut out each animal and laminate for durability.

2. Make copies of the zoo animal habitats from the pattern pages. Color, cut out, and laminate. Place each animal word flash card on the appropriate animal habitat.

3. Tape the animals randomly on the board.

4. Tell the children that the animals are loose and running amok. You need the children's help to get the animals back in the proper cage.

5. Have the children come up one at a time and select an animal from the board. Have each child name the animal ("This is a tiger."), tell something about the animal ("Tigers have stripes."), and place it in the proper zoo cage.

6. Continue until all of the animals are restored to the proper cages.

Extension: Have the children pick an animal from the zoo by listening to a short description and then matching it to the animal. Some suggestions to get you started:

- I like to sleep while standing on one leg.
- I like to pound my chest and swing in the trees.

If I Lived in the Zoo

Materials: paper, markers, 1/2" strips of black construction paper, glue

1. Have the children write or dictate a story about what kind of animal they would be if they lived at the zoo and why? What kinds of things would they do every day?

2. Have the children color a picture of an animal (or cut one from the "Animals" pattern pages) and put their face on it.

3. Tell the children to glue the construction paper strips over the top of their picture, leaving space in between the strips to make bars on the cage.

Create a Zoo

Materials: "Animals" pattern pages (pages 139–144), crayons, large sheet of manila construction paper, scissors, glue

1. Provide several copies of the pattern pages.

2. Have the children color and cut out as many animals as they wish.

3. Color and cut out the animal habitats for the children to use or have the children create their own zoo by drawing spaces for keeping the animals.

4. Reverse the project and provide the animal habitats. Have the children draw in their own animals at their zoo.

Check for Understanding

- There are many different kinds of animals.
- We can distinguish between different animals based on their individual characteristics.

0-7682-2810-7 *Learning Basic Vocabulary*

Name _____

Animals—Mammals

giraffe

bear

elephant

lion

DO NOT FEED ANIMALS

grassy plain

KEEP OFF FENCE

0-7682-2810-7 *Learning Basic Vocabulary*

Name_____

Animals—Reptiles

snake

alligator

lizard

turtle

desert

Name_____

Animals—Amphibians

toad

frog

caecilian

salamander

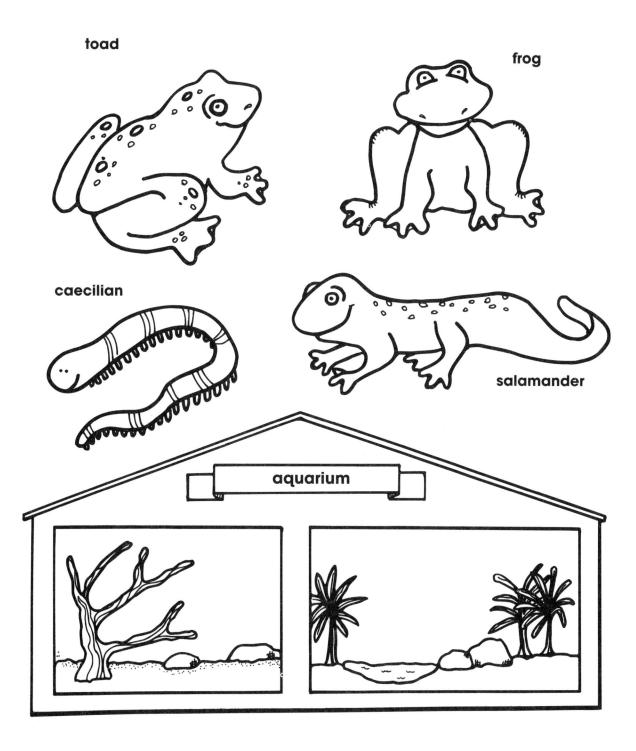

aquarium

0-7682-2810-7 *Learning Basic Vocabulary*

Name_____

Animals—Fish

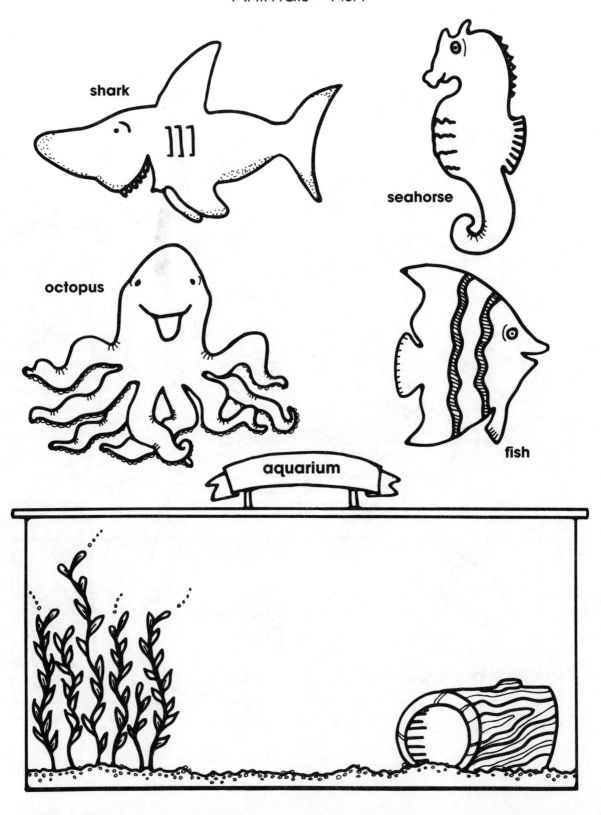

shark

seahorse

octopus

fish

aquarium

0-7682-2810-7 *Learning Basic Vocabulary*

Name _____

Animals—Birds

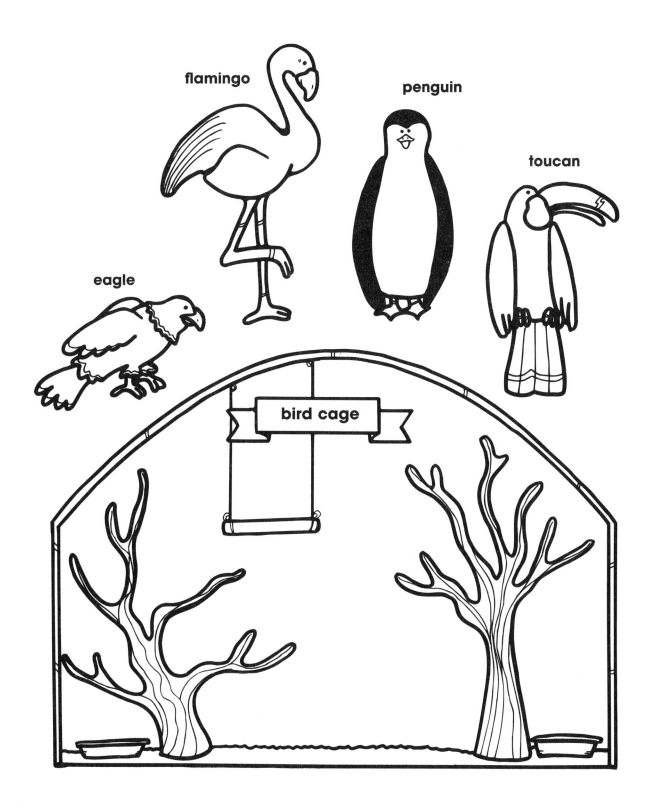

flamingo

penguin

toucan

eagle

bird cage

0-7682-2810-7 *Learning Basic Vocabulary*

Name _____

Animals—Insects

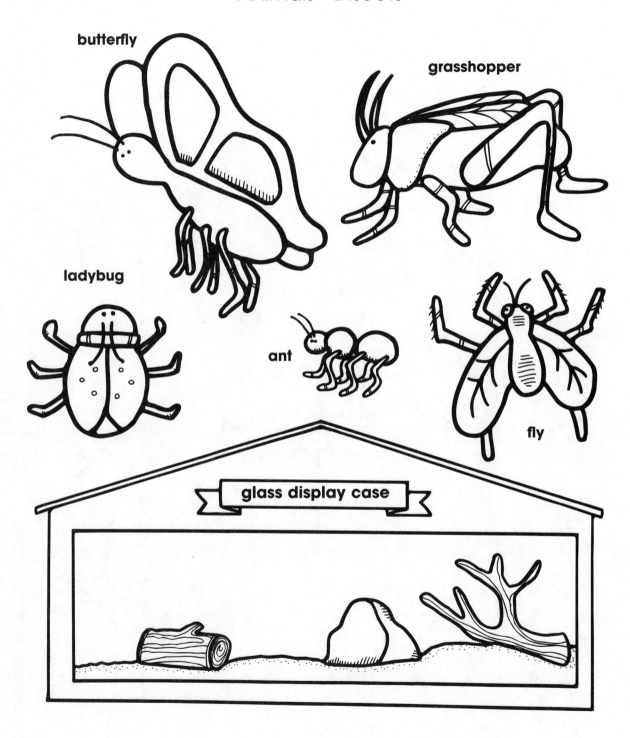

butterfly

grasshopper

ladybug

ant

fly

glass display case

0-7682-2810-7 *Learning Basic Vocabulary*

head

arm

elbow

hand

hip

leg

knee

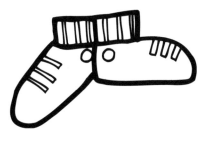

foot

sad

happy

proud

anxious

angry

surprised

frightened

bored

post office

store

fire station

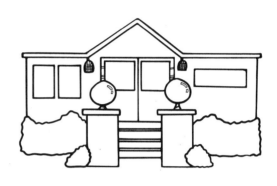

police station

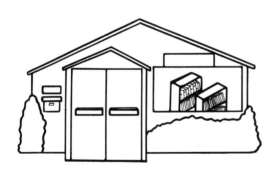

library

park

city hall

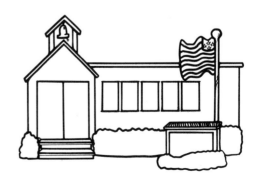

school

quarter

eight

dime

ten

penny

nine

nickel

dollar

one

five

two

six

three

seven

four

red

purple

blue

yellow

orange

black

white

green

sphere

cube

circle

square

triangle

rectangle

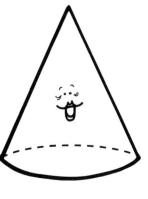

cone

cylinder

Sunday

Thursday

Monday

Friday

Tuesday

Saturday

Wednesday

week

January

May

February

June

March

July

April

August

September

spring

October

summer

November

autumn

December

winter

cold

sunny

hot

snowy

windy

cloudy

foggy

rainy

mammal

amphibian

bird

fish

insect

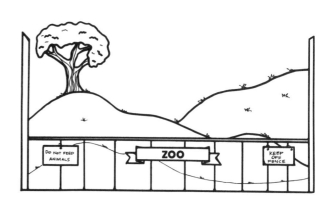

zoo

reptile

animal